Mediterranean Air Fryer Cookbook for Beginners:

1500 Days of Easy-to-Make Mediterranean Diet Recipes for Healthy and Quick Meals Every Day

Table of Contents

Breakfast Recipes 7
   Feta Eggs 7
   Yogurt Pancakes 7
   Garlic Omelet 8
   Paprika Lentils 8
   Cinnamon Oat Bars 9
   Almond Pudding 9
   Garlic Muffins 10
   Feta and Quinoa 10
   Cumin Tortillas 11
   Onion and Eggs 12
   Oregano Sandwich 13
   Fragrant Frittata 13
   Spinach and Oregano Sandwich 15
   Cinnamon Couscous 15
   Zucchini and Almond Muffins 16
   Yogurt Muffins 16
   Chicken and Eggs Sandwich 14
   Tomatoes Frittata 11
   Parsley Toast 14
   Eggs and Cheese 12

Fish and Seafood 18
   Paprika Cod 18
   Garlic Squid Rings 19
   Oregano Tilapia 21
   Lemon Seabass 19
   Garlic Scallops 18
   Onion and Basil Fish 19
   Bell Pepper and Mackerel 22
   Parsley Tapas 20
   Hummus Wraps 28
   Parmesan Tilapia 21
   Lemon Shrimps 22
   Tuna and Olives 23

- Oregano Catfish ... 23
- Garlic Cod ... 23
- Wine Mussels ... 25
- Honey Halibut ... 25
- Garlic Lobster Tail ... 24
- Oregano Swordfish ... 26
- Sweet Salmon ... 26
- Garlic Crab Cakes ... 27

Poultry & Meat ... 29
- Garlic Chicken ... 29
- Paprika Chicken Wings ... 29
- Oregano Chicken Drumsticks ... 30
- Tender Onion Chicken Breast ... 30
- Lemon and Garlic Beef Steak ... 31
- Spiced Beef Slices ... 31
- Aromatic Chicken Thighs ... 32
- Fragrant Pork Steak ... 32
- Garlic Pork Loin ... 33
- Sweet Lamb Ribs ... 33
- Tomatoes Meatballs ... 34
- Lemon Lamb Cutlets ... 34
- Tender Grilled Chicken ... 35
- Oregano Medallions ... 35
- Garlic Leg of Lamb ... 36
- Pepper Meat Mince ... 36
- Onion Chorizo ... 37
- Thyme Jerk Chicken ... 37
- Red Onion Chicken Skewers ... 38
- Parsley Chicken Patties ... 38

Vegetables ... 39
- Thyme Beets ... 39
- Paprika Broccoli ... 41
- Garlic Cauliflower Florets ... 39
- Tender Asparagus ... 39
- Lemon Artichoke ... 42

- Cinnamon Carrots 43
- Onion Potatoes 43
- Oregano Snap Peas 44
- Cumin Butternut Squash 44
- Greek Style Kalamata Olives 39
- Honey Apple Wedges 45
- Oregano Zucchini Sticks 46
- Garlic Mushroom Caps 46
- Thyme Eggplant 47
- Feta Beets 47
- Garlic Carrots 48
- Cumin Avocado Cubes 49
- Paprika Okra 40
- Paprika Corn 40
- Thyme Cabbage 48

Bread and Pizza 50
- Cherry Tomatoes Pizza 50
- Hummus Flatbread 50
- Basil Pizza 56
- Garlic Bread 57
- Blueberries Pizza 51
- Basil Pinwheels 51
- Walnuts Bread 52
- Cheese Flatbread 52
- Mozzarella Tart 53
- Olives Pizza 54
- Feta Pizza 54
- Tender Pizza 55
- Yogurt Bread 55
- Plain Bread 56
- Honey Bread 53

Pasta 58
- Basil Pasta 64
- Marinara Pasta 65
- Olives and Pasta 65

- Greens Pasta ... 58
- Tender Ravioli with Olives ... 58
- Oregano Pasta ... 59
- Fish Pasta ... 59
- Spaghetti & Parsley Meatballs ... 60
- Parmesan Pasta ... 61
- Tender Pasta with Olives ... 62
- Mushrooms and Oregano Pasta ... 60
- Italian Style Pasta ... 62
- Aromatic Ravioli with Tomatoes ... 60
- Seafood Pasta ... 63
- Zucchini and Pasta ... 63

Rice and Grains ... 67
- Mussels Paella ... 67
- Green Rice ... 67
- Tender Rice and Beef Balls ... 70
- Eggplant Rice ... 68
- Garlic Rice ... 68
- Oregano and Onion Bulgur ... 69
- Garlic Bulgur ... 69
- Paprika Bulgur ... 75
- Cumin Buckwheat ... 70
- Onion and Mushrooms Quinoa ... 74
- Bell Peppers Pilaf ... 70
- Tender Quinoa ... 71
- Paprika Quinoa Balls ... 71
- Garlic Sorghum ... 72
- Parlsey Farro ... 72
- Cumin Balls ... 75
- Thyme Rice ... 76
- Berries Quinoa ... 77
- Cheese Buckwheat ... 73
- Vegan Pilaf ... 73

Beans ... 78
- Onion Beans ... 78

Peppers and Beans Mix 78
Thyme Beans 79
Honey Snap Peas 79
Greek Style White Beans 80
Olives and Beans.. 80
Tender Bean Mash... 81
Oregano Canellini Beans.. 81
Paprika Black Beans Ragout... 82
Tomato Beans.. 82

Breakfast Recipes

Feta Eggs

Yield: 2 servings | **Prep time:** 10 minutes | **Cook time:** 15 minutes

Ingredients:

- 4 large eggs
- 2 medium-sized tomatoes, sliced
- 1/4 cup crumbled feta cheese
- 2 tablespoons chopped fresh parsley
- 1 tablespoon olive oil
- 1/4 teaspoon salt
- 1/4 teaspoon black pepper

Directions:

1. Preheat the air fryer to 350°F (175°C).
2. In a small bowl, whisk the eggs with the salt and pepper until well combined.
3. Grease the air fryer basket with the olive oil.
4. Place the sliced tomatoes in a single layer in the basket.
5. Pour the egg mixture over the tomatoes.
6. Sprinkle the crumbled feta cheese and chopped parsley over the eggs.
7. Air fry for 15 minutes, or until the eggs are set and the cheese is melted and golden brown.

Nutritional information: 217 calories, 13g protein, 8g carbohydrates, 15g fat, 2g fiber, 373mg cholesterol, 448mg sodium, 503mg potassium.

Yogurt Pancakes

Yield: 2 servings | **Prep time:** 10 minutes | **Cook time:** 10 minutes

Ingredients:

- 1 cup all-purpose flour
- 1 tablespoon sugar
- 1 teaspoon baking powder
- 1/4 teaspoon baking soda
- 1/4 teaspoon salt
- 1/2 cup plain Greek yogurt
- 1/2 cup milk
- 1 large egg
- 1 teaspoon vanilla extract

Directions:

1. In a medium bowl, whisk together the flour, sugar, baking powder, baking soda, and salt.
2. In another bowl, whisk together the yogurt, milk, egg, and vanilla extract until well combined.
3. Add the wet ingredients to the dry ingredients and whisk until just combined (the batter will be thick).
4. Preheat the air fryer to 350°F (175°C).
5. Grease the air fryer basket with cooking spray or oil.
6. Scoop the batter into the air fryer using a 1/4 cup measuring cup.
7. Air fry for 5 minutes on one side, then flip and air fry for another 3-5 minutes, or until the pancakes are golden brown and cooked through.

Nutritional information: 361 calories, 16g protein, 60g carbohydrates, 6g fat, 2g fiber, 98mg cholesterol, 764mg sodium, 393mg potassium.

Garlic Omelet

Yield: 2 servings | **Prep time:** 10 minutes | **Cook time:** 10 minutes

Ingredients:

- 4 large eggs
- 2 tablespoons milk
- 1/4 teaspoon salt
- 1/4 teaspoon black pepper
- 1/4 teaspoon garlic powder
- 1/2 cup marinated artichoke hearts, drained and chopped, low-sodium
- 1/4 cup crumbled feta cheese
- 1 tablespoon chopped fresh parsley

Directions:

1. In a medium bowl, whisk together the eggs, milk, salt, black pepper, and garlic powder.
2. Stir in the chopped artichoke hearts and feta cheese.
3. Preheat the air fryer to 375°F (190°C).
4. Grease the air fryer basket with cooking spray or oil.
5. Pour the egg mixture into the air fryer basket.
6. Air fry for 5 minutes, then use a spatula to gently lift and fold the omelet in half.
7. Air fry for an additional 3-5 minutes, or until the omelet is cooked through and golden brown.
8. Garnish with chopped parsley before serving.

Nutritional information: 210 calories, 17g protein, 4g carbohydrates, 14g fat, 1g fiber, 371mg cholesterol, 575mg sodium, 196mg potassium.

Paprika Lentils

Yield: 2 servings | **Prep time:** 10 minutes | **Cook time:** 15 minutes

Ingredients:

- 1/2 cup green lentils
- 1/2 cup water
- 1/2 tsp ground cinnamon
- 1/2 tsp ground cumin
- 1/2 tsp smoked paprika
- 1/2 tsp garlic powder
- 1 medium apple, peeled and diced
- 2 large eggs
- Salt and pepper, to taste

Directions:

1. Rinse the lentils and place them in the air fryer basket.
2. Add the water, cinnamon, cumin, smoked paprika, and garlic powder. Mix well.
3. Set the air fryer to 375°F and cook for 12-15 minutes, or until the lentils are tender and fully cooked.
4. Remove the lentils from the air fryer and add the diced apple. Mix well and set aside.
5. In a small bowl, whisk the eggs with salt and pepper.
6. Pour the eggs into the air fryer basket and set the air fryer to 350°F.
7. Cook the eggs for 3-4 minutes, or until set and fully cooked.
8. Serve the cooked lentils with the scrambled eggs on top.

Nutritional information: 223 calories, 14g protein, 33g carbohydrates, 3g fat, 7g fiber, 186mg cholesterol, 80mg sodium, 665mg potassium.

Cinnamon Oat Bars

Yield: 6 bars | **Prep time:** 10 minutes | **Cook time:** 15 minutes

Ingredients:

- 1 cup rolled oats
- 1/2 cup almond flour
- 1/4 cup honey
- 1/4 cup unsweetened applesauce
- 1/4 cup chopped walnuts
- 1/4 cup raisins
- 1 tsp cinnamon
- 1/2 tsp vanilla extract
- Pinch of salt

Directions:

1. Preheat the air fryer to 350°F (180°C).
2. In a mixing bowl, combine the oats, almond flour, cinnamon, and salt.
3. Add the honey, unsweetened applesauce, vanilla extract, walnuts, and raisins to the mixing bowl, and mix well.
4. Line an 8x8 inch (20x20 cm) baking dish with parchment paper.
5. Pour the oat mixture into the lined baking dish and press it down with your hands to form an even layer.
6. Place the baking dish in the air fryer basket and cook for 15 minutes, or until the edges are golden brown.
7. Remove the baking dish from the air fryer and let it cool for 10 minutes before slicing into 6 bars.

Nutritional information: 218 calories, 6g protein, 28g carbohydrates, 10g fat, 4g fiber, 0mg cholesterol, 20mg sodium, 194mg potassium.

Almond Pudding

Yield: 4 servings | **Prep time:** 10 minutes | **Cook time:** 20 minutes

Ingredients:

- 1/2 cup chopped walnuts
- 1/2 cup rolled oats
- 1/2 cup almond milk
- 2 tablespoons maple syrup
- 1 teaspoon vanilla extract
- 1/4 teaspoon ground cinnamon

Directions:

1. Preheat your air fryer to 350°F (180°C).
2. In a mixing bowl, combine the chopped walnuts, rolled oats, almond milk, maple syrup, vanilla extract, and ground cinnamon. Mix well.
3. Pour the mixture into a greased baking dish that fits inside your air fryer basket.
4. Place the baking dish in the air fryer basket and cook for 20 minutes.
5. Once done, remove from the air fryer and let cool for a few minutes before serving.

Nutritional information: 230 calories, 6g protein, 21g carbohydrates, 14g fat, 4g fiber, 0mg cholesterol, 20mg sodium, 220mg potassium.

Garlic Muffins

Yield: 6 servings | **Prep time:** 15 minutes | **Cook time:** 10 minutes

Ingredients:

- 1 can tuna, drained and flaked
- 2 eggs
- 1/4 cup almond flour
- 1/4 cup chopped red onion
- 1/4 cup chopped roasted red peppers
- 1/4 cup chopped fresh parsley
- 1/2 tsp. dried oregano
- 1/2 tsp. garlic powder
- Salt and pepper to taste

Directions:

1. In a mixing bowl, whisk together eggs, almond flour, red onion, roasted red peppers, parsley, oregano, garlic powder, salt, and pepper.
2. Add the tuna and stir well.
3. Preheat the air fryer to 375°F (190°C).
4. Grease a muffin tin with cooking spray or line with silicone muffin cups.
5. Spoon the tuna mixture into the muffin cups.
6. Air fry the muffins for 10 minutes or until the tops are golden brown and the muffins are cooked through.
7. Serve warm or at room temperature.

Nutritional information: 105 calories, 11g protein, 2g carbohydrates, 6g fat, 1g fiber, 105mg cholesterol, 217mg sodium, 173mg potassium.

Feta and Quinoa

Yield: 2 servings | **Prep time:** 5 minutes | **Cook time:** 15 minutes

Ingredients:

- 1/2 cup uncooked quinoa
- 1 cup water
- 1/4 cup sliced almonds
- 1/4 cup chopped dried apricots
- 1/4 cup crumbled feta cheese
- 1 tbsp extra-virgin olive oil
- Salt and pepper, to taste

Directions:

1. Rinse the quinoa in a fine-mesh sieve under running water.
2. In a medium bowl, add the quinoa and water. Mix well and transfer to the air fryer basket.
3. Cook for 10 minutes at 350°F.
4. After 10 minutes, remove the basket and stir the quinoa. Add the sliced almonds and dried apricots.
5. Return the basket to the air fryer and cook for an additional 5 minutes at 350°F.
6. Once done, remove from the air fryer and drizzle with olive oil. Season with salt and pepper to taste.
7. Top with crumbled feta cheese and serve.

Nutritional information: 309 calories, 10g protein, 34g carbohydrates, 16g fat, 5g fiber, 8mg cholesterol, 135mg sodium, 381mg potassium.

Cumin Tortillas

Yield: 2 servings | **Prep time:** 15 minutes | **Cook time:** 10 minutes

Ingredients:

- 2 small chicken breasts, cut into strips
- 1 tablespoon olive oil
- 1/2 teaspoon paprika
- 1/2 teaspoon ground cumin
- Salt and black pepper, to taste
- 2 whole wheat tortillas
- 1/4 cup chopped fresh parsley
- 1/4 cup chopped fresh mint
- 1/2 cup chopped cucumber
- 1/2 cup diced tomato
- 2 tablespoons crumbled feta cheese

Directions:

1. Preheat the air fryer to 375°F (190°C).
2. In a small bowl, mix together the olive oil, paprika, cumin, salt, and pepper. Add the chicken strips and toss to coat.
3. Place the chicken strips in the air fryer basket and cook for 8-10 minutes, or until cooked through and golden brown.
4. Meanwhile, warm the tortillas in the microwave or on a griddle.
5. In a small bowl, mix together the parsley, mint, cucumber, and tomato.
6. Assemble the tortillas by placing the cooked chicken strips on top of the warm tortillas. Top with the herb and vegetable mixture and sprinkle with crumbled feta cheese.
7. Serve immediately and enjoy!

Nutritional information: 402 calories, 36g protein, 25g carbohydrates, 18g fat, 6g fiber, 91mg cholesterol, 693mg sodium, 756mg potassium.

Tomatoes Frittata

Yield: 2 servings | **Prep time:** 10 minutes | **Cook time:** 15 minutes

Ingredients:

- 4 eggs
- 1/4 cup milk
- 1/4 cup crumbled feta cheese
- 1/4 cup diced tomatoes
- 1/4 cup sliced mushrooms
- 1/4 cup chopped fresh spinach
- Salt and pepper to taste

Directions:

1. In a bowl, beat eggs and milk together. Add feta cheese and mix well.
2. Add diced tomatoes, sliced mushrooms, and chopped fresh spinach to the mixture.
3. Season with salt and pepper and stir to combine.
4. Pour the mixture into an air fryer-safe dish and place in the air fryer basket.
5. Air fry at 350°F for 15 minutes or until the frittata is set and the top is golden brown.
6. Remove the dish from the air fryer and let it cool for a few minutes before serving.

Nutritional information: 191 calories, 15g protein, 4g carbohydrates, 13g fat, 1g fiber, 359mg cholesterol, 365mg sodium, 340mg potassium.

Onion and Eggs

Yield: 2 servings | **Prep time:** 10 minutes | **Cook time:** 15 minutes

Ingredients:

- 1 red bell pepper, sliced
- 1 yellow bell pepper, sliced
- 1 zucchini, sliced
- 1 small red onion, sliced
- 4 large eggs
- 2 tablespoons olive oil
- 1 teaspoon dried oregano
- Salt and black pepper to taste

Directions:

1. Preheat the air fryer to 375°F (190°C).
2. In a mixing bowl, combine the sliced red bell pepper, yellow bell pepper, zucchini, and red onion. Add olive oil, dried oregano, salt, and black pepper, and toss to coat.
3. Transfer the vegetables to the air fryer basket and cook for 12-15 minutes or until the vegetables are tender and lightly charred, stirring halfway through.
4. Crack the eggs on top of the vegetables in the air fryer basket, making sure to space them apart. Sprinkle some salt and black pepper on top of the eggs.
5. Return the basket to the air fryer and cook for an additional 3-5 minutes, depending on how well-done you want your eggs.
6. Carefully remove the basket from the air fryer and serve the vegetables and eggs immediately.

Nutritional information: 259 calories, 12g protein, 14g carbohydrates, 19g fat, 4g fiber, 377mg cholesterol, 139mg sodium, 844mg potassium.

Eggs and Cheese

Yield: 2 servings | **Prep time:** 5 minutes | **Cook time:** 10 minutes

Ingredients:

- 4 large eggs
- 1/4 cup crumbled feta cheese
- 1/4 cup Kalamata olives, pitted and chopped
- 1/4 cup chopped fresh parsley
- 1/4 teaspoon dried oregano
- Salt and pepper to taste

Directions:

1. In a mixing bowl, whisk together the eggs, feta cheese, Kalamata olives, parsley, oregano, salt, and pepper until well combined.
2. Preheat the air fryer to 350°F (175°C).
3. Pour the egg mixture into a lightly greased air fryer basket.
4. Cook for 10 minutes or until the eggs are set and the top is lightly golden.
5. Carefully remove the basket from the air fryer and let the eggs cool for a few minutes before slicing and serving.

Nutritional information: 199 calories, 15g protein, 3g carbohydrates, 14g fat, 1g fiber, 373mg cholesterol, 605mg sodium, 174mg potassium.

Oregano Sandwich

Yield: 2 servings | **Prep time:** 10 minutes | **Cook time:** 10 minutes

Ingredients:

- 4 slices of bread
- 2 eggs
- 2 tablespoons crumbled feta cheese
- 1 tablespoon chopped fresh parsley
- 1/2 teaspoon dried oregano
- 1/4 teaspoon garlic powder
- Salt and pepper to taste
- Cooking spray

Directions:

1. Preheat the air fryer to 375°F (190°C).
2. In a small bowl, whisk together the eggs, feta cheese, parsley, oregano, garlic powder, salt, and pepper.
3. Spray the air fryer basket with cooking spray and place the bread slices in a single layer in the basket.
4. Pour the egg mixture over the bread, making sure it's evenly distributed.
5. Place the basket in the air fryer and cook for 8-10 minutes, or until the eggs are set and the bread is toasted to your liking.
6. Remove from the air fryer, slice in half, and serve hot.

Nutritional information: 293 calories, 16g protein, 25g carbohydrates, 13g fat, 1g fiber, 202mg cholesterol, 479mg sodium, 197mg potassium.

Fragrant Frittata

Yield: 2 servings | **Prep time:** 10 minutes | **Cook time:** 15 minutes

Ingredients:

- 4 large eggs
- 2 tablespoons milk
- 1/4 teaspoon salt
- 1/4 teaspoon black pepper
- 1 tablespoon olive oil
- 1/4 cup diced onion
- 1/4 cup chopped fresh spinach
- 1/4 cup crumbled feta cheese

Directions:

1. In a mixing bowl, whisk together the eggs, milk, salt, and black pepper.
2. Heat the olive oil in a small skillet over medium heat. Add the onions and sauté until they are soft, about 3 minutes.
3. Add the spinach to the skillet and sauté until it wilts, about 2 minutes.
4. Pour the egg mixture into the skillet and stir gently to combine.
5. Cook for 8-10 minutes in the air fryer at 350°F until the frittata is set and the top is golden brown.
6. Remove the frittata from the air fryer and sprinkle with the crumbled feta cheese.
7. Cut into slices and serve hot.

Nutritional information: 218 calories, 15g protein, 4g carbohydrates, 16g fat, 1g fiber, 360mg cholesterol, 487mg sodium, 241mg potassium.

Chicken and Eggs Sandwich

Yield: 2 servings | **Prep time:** 10 minutes | **Cook time:** 15 minutes

Ingredients:

- 2 boneless, skinless chicken breasts
- 1 teaspoon dried oregano
- 1 teaspoon dried thyme
- 1/2 teaspoon garlic powder
- Salt and black pepper, to taste
- 1 tablespoon olive oil
- 2 English muffins, split and toasted
- 2 large eggs, scrambled
- 2 slices of feta cheese
- 2 tablespoons chopped fresh parsley

Directions:

1. Preheat the air fryer to 400°F (200°C).
2. Season the chicken breasts with oregano, thyme, garlic powder, salt, and pepper.
3. Drizzle olive oil over the chicken breasts and toss to coat.
4. Place the chicken in the air fryer basket and cook for 12-15 minutes, flipping halfway through, or until the internal temperature reaches 165°F (75°C).
5. Assemble the sandwich by placing a chicken breast on each toasted English muffin half.
6. Top each chicken breast with scrambled eggs, feta cheese, and chopped parsley.
7. Serve immediately.

Nutritional information: 427 calories, 38g protein, 27g carbohydrates, 18g fat, 2g fiber, 292mg cholesterol, 625mg sodium, 555mg potassium.

Parsley Toast

Yield: 2 servings | **Prep time:** 5 minutes | **Cook time:** 5 minutes

Ingredients:

- 2 slices of whole-grain bread
- 2 large eggs
- 1/4 cup of crumbled feta cheese
- 1/2 cup of cherry tomatoes, halved
- 1 tablespoon of chopped fresh parsley
- Salt and pepper to taste
- Olive oil spray

Directions:

1. Preheat your air fryer to 350°F (180°C).
2. Crack one egg into each of two separate small bowls or ramekins.
3. Spray the air fryer basket with olive oil.
4. Place one slice of bread in the air fryer basket and pour one egg onto the bread, then sprinkle with feta cheese and tomatoes.
5. Place the second slice of bread on top of the first and pour the second egg onto the bread, then sprinkle with feta cheese and tomatoes.
6. Air fry for 5 minutes or until the eggs are set and the toast is crispy.
7. Sprinkle with chopped parsley and salt and pepper to taste.

Nutritional information: 314 calories, 19g protein, 23g carbohydrates, 16g fat, 5g fiber, 400mg cholesterol, 569mg sodium, 351mg potassium.

Spinach and Oregano Sandwich

Yield: 2 servings | **Prep time:** 10 minutes | **Cook time:** 10 minutes

Ingredients:

- 2 small fillets of white fish (such as cod or tilapia)
- 1/4 cup all-purpose flour
- 1/4 cup breadcrumbs
- 1/2 tsp garlic powder
- 1/2 tsp dried oregano
- Salt and pepper to taste
- 2 whole wheat buns
- 1/2 cup baby spinach leaves
- 2 tbsp plain Greek yogurt
- 1 tbsp lemon juice
- 1 tbsp olive oil

Directions:

1. Preheat the air fryer to 375°F (190°C).
2. In a shallow dish, mix together the flour, breadcrumbs, garlic powder, oregano, salt, and pepper.
3. Dip the fish fillets into the flour mixture, shaking off any excess.
4. Place the fish fillets into the air fryer basket and spray them with cooking spray.
5. Cook for 8-10 minutes, until the fish is cooked through and golden brown.
6. While the fish is cooking, mix together the Greek yogurt, lemon juice, and olive oil in a small bowl.
7. Toast the buns and spread the yogurt sauce on the bottom bun.
8. Top each bun with spinach leaves and a cooked fish fillet.
9. Serve immediately and enjoy!

Nutritional information: 394 calories, 30g protein, 36g carbohydrates, 14g fat, 5g fiber, 59mg cholesterol, 482mg sodium, 660mg potassium.

Cinnamon Couscous

Yield: 2 servings | **Prep time:** 10 minutes | **Cook time:** 10 minutes

Ingredients:

- 1/2 cup couscous
- 3/4 cup water
- 1/4 tsp salt
- 1/2 tsp cinnamon
- 1/2 tsp honey
- 1/2 cup chopped mixed fruits (such as apple, banana, and berries)
- 1 tbsp chopped nuts (such as almonds or walnuts)
- 1 tbsp raisins
- 1 tbsp Greek yogurt (optional)

Directions:

1. Preheat the air fryer to 360°F.
2. In a small pot, bring the water and salt to a boil. Stir in the couscous, cover, and remove from heat. Let stand for 5 minutes.
3. Fluff the couscous with a fork and stir in the cinnamon, honey, chopped fruits, nuts, and raisins.

4. Transfer the couscous mixture to an air fryer basket and spread it out in an even layer.
5. Air fry for 5 minutes, shaking the basket occasionally, until the couscous is lightly toasted.
6. Serve hot with a dollop of Greek yogurt, if desired.

Nutritional information: 238 calories, 6g protein, 48g carbohydrates, 3g fat, 5g fiber, 0mg cholesterol, 305mg sodium, 332mg potassium.

Zucchini and Almond Muffins

Yield: 6 muffins | **Prep time:** 10 minutes | **Cook time**: 15 minutes

Ingredients:

- 1 medium zucchini, grated
- 1/2 cup whole wheat flour
- 1/2 cup almond flour
- 1 tsp baking powder
- 1/4 tsp salt
- 2 eggs
- 1/4 cup olive oil
- 1/4 cup honey
- 1/4 cup crumbled feta cheese

Directions:

1. Preheat the air fryer to 350°F (180°C).
2. In a large bowl, combine the grated zucchini, whole wheat flour, almond flour, baking powder, and salt.
3. In a separate bowl, whisk together the eggs, olive oil, and honey.
4. Add the wet ingredients to the dry ingredients and mix until well combined.
5. Fold in the crumbled feta cheese.
6. Spoon the batter into a greased muffin tin, filling each muffin cup about 3/4 full.
7. Place the muffin tin in the air fryer basket and cook for 15 minutes, or until a toothpick inserted into the center of a muffin comes out clean.
8. Let the muffins cool for a few minutes before removing them from the muffin tin.

Nutritional information: 213 calories, 6g protein, 18g carbohydrates, 13g fat, 2g fiber, 71mg cholesterol, 203mg sodium, 154mg potassium.

Yogurt Muffins

Yield: 6 muffins | **Prep time:** 10 minutes | **Cook time**: 12 minutes

Ingredients:

- 1 cup all-purpose flour
- 1/4 cup sugar
- 1 tsp baking powder
- 1/4 tsp baking soda
- 1/4 tsp salt
- 1/2 cup plain Greek yogurt
- 1 egg
- 1/4 cup unsweetened almond milk
- 1 cup mixed berries (such as blueberries, raspberries, and blackberries)

Directions:

1. Preheat the air fryer to 350°F (180°C).
2. In a mixing bowl, whisk together the flour, sugar, baking powder, baking soda, and salt.

3. In a separate bowl, beat the Greek yogurt, egg, and almond milk until smooth.
4. Add the wet mixture to the dry mixture and stir until just combined.
5. Gently fold in the mixed berries.
6. Grease a muffin tin or line with muffin cups.
7. Spoon the batter into the muffin cups, filling each about 3/4 full.
8. Place the muffin tin into the air fryer basket and cook for 10-12 minutes, or until a toothpick inserted into the center of a muffin comes out clean.
9. Let the muffins cool for a few minutes before serving.

Nutritional information: 121 calories, 4g protein, 23g carbohydrates, 2g fat, 2g fiber, 28mg cholesterol, 213mg sodium, 107mg potassium.

Fish and Seafood

Paprika Cod

Yield: 2 servings | **Prep time:** 10 minutes | **Cook time:** 12 minutes

Ingredients:

- 2 cod fillets (about 6 oz each)
- 1/4 cup all-purpose flour
- 1/2 tsp garlic powder
- 1/2 tsp smoked paprika
- 1/2 tsp dried oregano
- 1/4 tsp salt
- 1/4 tsp black pepper
- 1 tbsp olive oil
- 1 lemon, sliced

Directions:

1. Preheat the air fryer to 400°F.
2. In a shallow bowl, mix together the flour, garlic powder, smoked paprika, dried oregano, salt, and black pepper.
3. Dip each cod fillet into the flour mixture, making sure it's coated evenly.
4. Drizzle olive oil over the cod fillets and place them in the air fryer basket.
5. Top each fillet with lemon slices.
6. Air fry the cod fillets for 12 minutes, flipping halfway through the cooking time.
7. Serve hot.

Nutritional information: 250 calories, 32g protein, 13g carbohydrates, 8g fat, 2g fiber, 72mg cholesterol, 358mg sodium, 613mg potassium.

Garlic Scallops

Yield: 2 servings | **Prep time:** 10 minutes | **Cook time:** 10 minutes

Ingredients:

- 1/2 lb scallops
- 1 tbsp olive oil
- 1 tsp smoked paprika
- 1/2 tsp garlic powder
- 1/2 tsp salt
- 1/4 tsp black pepper

Directions:

1. Preheat the air fryer to 400°F (200°C).
2. In a small bowl, mix together olive oil, smoked paprika, garlic powder, salt, and black pepper.
3. Pat the scallops dry with a paper towel.
4. Brush both sides of each scallop with the spice mixture.
5. Place the scallops in a single layer in the air fryer basket.
6. Cook for 6-8 minutes, or until the scallops are cooked through and lightly browned on the outside.
7. Serve immediately with lemon wedges.

Nutritional information: 130 calories, 23g protein, 1g carbohydrates, 4g fat, 0g fiber, 47mg cholesterol, 443mg sodium, 340mg potassium.

Lemon Seabass

Yield: 2 servings | **Prep time:** 10 minutes | **Cook time:** 12 minutes

Ingredients:

- 2 seabass fillets, skin on
- 1 tablespoon olive oil
- 1 tablespoon lemon juice
- 1 tablespoon chopped fresh thyme leaves
- 1 teaspoon garlic powder
- 1/2 teaspoon sea salt
- 1/4 teaspoon black pepper

Directions:

1. Preheat the air fryer to 375°F.
2. In a small bowl, mix together the olive oil, lemon juice, thyme leaves, garlic powder, sea salt, and black pepper.
3. Pat the seabass fillets dry with a paper towel and place them skin-side down in the air fryer basket.
4. Brush the fillets with the herb mixture, making sure to coat them well.
5. Air fry for 10-12 minutes, or until the fish is cooked through and flakes easily with a fork.
6. Serve immediately, garnished with additional thyme leaves and lemon wedges if desired.

Nutritional information: 235 calories, 35g protein, 1g carbohydrates, 10g fat, 0g fiber, 90mg cholesterol, 410mg sodium, 620mg potassium.

Onion and Basil Fish

Yield: 2 servings | **Prep time:** 10 minutes | **Cook time:** 15 minutes

Ingredients:

- 2 tilapia fillets
- 2 tablespoons of olive oil
- 1 teaspoon of dried basil
- 1/2 teaspoon of garlic powder
- 1/2 teaspoon of onion powder
- 1/4 teaspoon of salt
- 1/4 teaspoon of black pepper
- 1 cup of cherry tomatoes, halved

Directions:

1. Preheat the air fryer to 400°F (200°C).
2. Rinse and pat dry the tilapia fillets.
3. In a small bowl, combine the olive oil, basil, garlic powder, onion powder, salt, and black pepper.
4. Brush the spice mixture over both sides of the tilapia fillets.
5. Place the seasoned fillets in the air fryer basket and add the cherry tomatoes around them.
6. Cook for 12-15 minutes, or until the tilapia is cooked through and the tomatoes are soft and slightly charred.
7. Serve hot and enjoy!

Nutritional information: 293 calories, 35g protein, 6g carbohydrates, 14g fat, 2g fiber, 75mg cholesterol, 341mg sodium, 758mg potassium.

Garlic Squid Rings

Yield: 2 servings | **Prep time:** 15 minutes | **Cook time:** 10 minutes

Ingredients:

- 1 lb squid rings
- 1/4 cup all-purpose flour
- 1/2 tsp garlic powder
- 1/2 tsp smoked paprika
- 1/4 tsp salt
- 1/4 tsp black pepper
- 1/4 cup panko breadcrumbs
- Cooking spray

Directions:

1. Preheat the air fryer to 400°F.
2. In a shallow dish, mix together the flour, garlic powder, smoked paprika, salt, and black pepper.
3. In another shallow dish, place the panko breadcrumbs.
4. Dredge the squid rings in the flour mixture, shaking off any excess.
5. Dip the squid rings into the panko breadcrumbs, pressing the breadcrumbs to adhere.
6. Spray the air fryer basket with cooking spray and place the squid rings in a single layer.
7. Cook in the air fryer for 8-10 minutes, flipping halfway through, until golden brown and crispy.
8. Serve with lemon wedges and your favorite dipping sauce.

Nutritional information: 225 calories, 26g protein, 19g carbohydrates, 4g fat, 1g fiber, 305mg cholesterol, 430mg sodium, 433mg potassium.

Parsley Tapas

Yield: 2 servings | **Prep time:** 10 minutes | **Cook time:** 8 minutes

Ingredients:

- 2 salmon fillets (4 oz each)
- 1 tbsp olive oil
- 1 tbsp smoked paprika
- 1 tsp garlic powder
- 1/2 tsp salt
- 1/4 tsp black pepper
- 1/4 cup chopped fresh parsley
- 1 lemon, cut into wedges

Directions:

1. Preheat the air fryer to 400°F (200°C).
2. In a small bowl, mix together the olive oil, smoked paprika, garlic powder, salt, and black pepper.
3. Rub the spice mixture onto the salmon fillets.
4. Place the salmon fillets in the air fryer basket and cook for 8 minutes.
5. Once cooked, remove the salmon from the air fryer basket and place on a serving plate.
6. Sprinkle with chopped fresh parsley and serve with lemon wedges.

Nutritional information: 235 calories, 29g protein, 2g carbohydrates, 13g fat, 1g fiber, 75mg cholesterol, 625mg sodium, 547mg potassium.

Oregano Tilapia

Yield: 2 servings | **Prep time:** 10 minutes | **Cook time:** 10 minutes

Ingredients:

- 2 tilapia fillets, cut into bite-sized pieces
- 1/2 cup panko breadcrumbs
- 1/4 cup grated Parmesan cheese
- 1 tsp dried oregano
- 1 tsp garlic powder
- 1/4 cup all-purpose flour
- 1 egg, beaten
- Salt and black pepper, to taste
- Olive oil cooking spray

Directions:

1. In a small bowl, mix together panko breadcrumbs, grated Parmesan cheese, dried oregano, garlic powder, and salt.
2. Place all-purpose flour and beaten egg in separate bowls.
3. Dip each tilapia bite into the flour, shaking off any excess, then dip into the beaten egg, and finally coat with the breadcrumb mixture.
4. Place the coated tilapia bites in a single layer in the air fryer basket.
5. Lightly spray the bites with olive oil cooking spray.
6. Air fry at 380°F for 10 minutes, flipping halfway through, until golden brown and crispy.
7. Serve hot with your favorite dipping sauce.

Nutritional information: 292 calories, 31g protein, 23g carbohydrates, 7g fat, 1g fiber, 120mg cholesterol, 289mg sodium, 422mg potassium.

Parmesan Tilapia

Yield: 2 servings | **Prep time:** 10 minutes | **Cook time:** 15 minutes

Ingredients:

- 2 tilapia fillets
- 1/2 cup plain Greek yogurt
- 1/4 cup breadcrumbs
- 1/4 cup grated Parmesan cheese
- 1 teaspoon dried oregano
- 1 teaspoon garlic powder
- Salt and black pepper, to taste
- Lemon wedges, for serving

Directions:

1. Preheat the air fryer to 375°F.
2. In a small bowl, mix together the Greek yogurt, breadcrumbs, Parmesan cheese, oregano, garlic powder, salt, and black pepper until well combined.
3. Dip each tilapia fillet into the yogurt mixture, making sure it is fully coated.
4. Place the coated fillets in the air fryer basket, making sure they are not overlapping.
5. Cook the tilapia fillets for 15 minutes, or until golden brown and cooked through.
6. Serve the air fryer yogurt tilapia with lemon wedges on the side.

Nutritional information: 261 calories, 36g protein, 9g carbohydrates, 8g fat, 1g fiber, 87mg cholesterol, 332mg sodium, 523mg potassium.

Bell Pepper and Mackerel

Yield: 2 servings | **Prep time:** 15 minutes | **Cook time:** 15 minutes

Ingredients:

- 2 medium-sized mackerel, gutted and cleaned
- 1/4 cup diced onion
- 1/4 cup diced tomato
- 1/4 cup diced bell pepper
- 2 cloves garlic, minced
- 2 tablespoons chopped fresh parsley
- 2 tablespoons olive oil
- Salt and pepper, to taste

Directions:

1. Preheat the air fryer to 360°F (182°C).
2. In a bowl, mix together the onion, tomato, bell pepper, garlic, parsley, olive oil, salt, and pepper.
3. Stuff each mackerel with the mixture and secure with toothpicks.
4. Place the stuffed mackerel in the air fryer basket and cook for 12-15 minutes, or until the fish is cooked through and flaky.
5. Remove from the air fryer and allow to cool for a few minutes before removing the toothpicks and serving.

Nutritional information: 313 calories, 27g protein, 4g carbohydrates, 22g fat, 1g fiber, 108mg cholesterol, 125mg sodium, 601mg potassium.

Lemon Shrimps

Yield: 2 servings | **Prep time:** 10 minutes | **Cook time:** 10 minutes

Ingredients:

- 1/2 lb raw shrimp, peeled and deveined
- 1 tbsp olive oil
- 1 tbsp lemon juice
- 2 cloves garlic, minced
- 1 tsp ground coriander
- 1/2 tsp paprika
- 1/2 tsp salt
- 1/4 tsp black pepper
- Fresh coriander leaves, chopped, for garnish

Directions:

1. In a medium-sized bowl, mix together olive oil, lemon juice, minced garlic, ground coriander, paprika, salt, and black pepper.
2. Add the raw shrimp to the bowl and toss well to coat with the marinade.
3. Preheat the air fryer to 400°F.
4. Place the marinated shrimp in a single layer in the air fryer basket.
5. Air fry the shrimp for 8-10 minutes or until they turn pink and are cooked through, flipping them halfway through.
6. Garnish with chopped fresh coriander leaves and serve.

Nutritional information: 132 calories, 20g protein, 2g carbohydrates, 5g fat, 0g fiber, 172mg cholesterol, 775mg sodium, 223mg potassium.

Oregano Catfish

Yield: 2 servings | **Prep time:** 10 minutes | **Cook time:** 12 minutes

Ingredients:

- 2 catfish fillets
- 1/4 cup all-purpose flour
- 1/4 cup panko breadcrumbs
- 1/4 cup grated parmesan cheese
- 1 tsp dried oregano
- 1/2 tsp garlic powder
- 1/2 tsp paprika
- Salt and pepper to taste
- Olive oil cooking spray

Directions:

1. Preheat the air fryer to 400°F (200°C).
2. In a bowl, mix together the flour, breadcrumbs, parmesan cheese, oregano, garlic powder, paprika, salt, and pepper.
3. Coat the catfish fillets in the breadcrumb mixture, pressing the mixture onto both sides of the fish.
4. Spray the air fryer basket with cooking spray and place the catfish fillets in the basket.
5. Spray the tops of the fillets with cooking spray.
6. Cook the catfish fillets in the air fryer for 12 minutes or until the internal temperature reaches 145°F (63°C).
7. Serve hot with lemon wedges and a side salad.

Nutritional information: 265 calories, 29g protein, 16g carbohydrates, 8g fat, 1g fiber, 89mg cholesterol, 239mg sodium, 391mg potassium.

Tuna and Olives

Yield: 2 servings | **Prep time:** 10 minutes | **Cook time:** 12 minutes

Ingredients:

- 2.6-ounce tuna steaks
- 1/4 cup crumbled feta cheese
- 1/4 cup cherry tomatoes, halved
- 1/4 cup chopped Kalamata olives
- 1 tablespoon chopped fresh parsley
- 1 tablespoon olive oil
- Salt and black pepper, to taste

Directions:

1. Preheat the air fryer to 400°F (200°C).
2. Season the tuna steaks with salt and black pepper, then brush them with olive oil.
3. Place the tuna steaks in the air fryer basket and cook for 6 minutes.
4. Remove the basket from the air fryer and sprinkle the feta cheese, cherry tomatoes, and Kalamata olives over the tuna steaks.
5. Return the basket to the air fryer and cook for an additional 6 minutes, or until the tuna is cooked through.
6. Serve the tuna steaks hot, garnished with chopped fresh parsley.

Nutritional information: 332 calories, 41g protein, 3g carbohydrates, 17g fat, 1g fiber, 97mg cholesterol, 727mg sodium, 567mg potassium.

Garlic Cod

Yield: 2 servings | **Prep time:** 10 minutes | **Cook time:** 10 minutes

Ingredients:

- 2 cod fillets
- 2 tablespoons teriyaki sauce
- 1 tablespoon honey
- 1 tablespoon rice vinegar
- 1 garlic clove, minced
- 1 teaspoon grated fresh ginger

Directions:

1. In a small bowl, whisk together the teriyaki sauce, honey, rice vinegar, minced garlic, and grated ginger until well combined.
2. Preheat the air fryer to 400°F.
3. Brush the teriyaki sauce mixture generously over both sides of the cod fillets.
4. Place the cod fillets in the air fryer basket and cook for 10 minutes, flipping halfway through cooking time, until the cod is cooked through and the outside is crispy.
5. Serve immediately and enjoy.

Nutritional information: 219 calories, 26g protein, 15g carbohydrates, 5g fat, 0g fiber, 50mg cholesterol, 766mg sodium, 418mg potassium.

Garlic Lobster Tail

Yield: 2 servings | **Prep time:** 10 minutes | **Cook time:** 10 minutes

Ingredients:

- 2 lobster tails, thawed
- 1/4 cup olive oil
- 1/4 cup lemon juice
- 2 garlic cloves, minced
- 1 teaspoon dried oregano
- 1/2 teaspoon salt
- 1/4 teaspoon black pepper

Directions:

1. Preheat the air fryer to 400°F (200°C).
2. Using kitchen shears, cut the top of the lobster shell down to the tail, being careful not to cut the meat.
3. Gently pull the meat out of the shell and place it on top of the shell.
4. In a small bowl, whisk together the olive oil, lemon juice, garlic, oregano, salt, and pepper.
5. Brush the lobster tails with the mixture, making sure to coat them evenly.
6. Place the lobster tails in the air fryer basket, meat side up.
7. Cook for 10 minutes, or until the lobster meat is opaque and the internal temperature reaches 145°F (63°C).
8. Serve with lemon wedges and additional sauce on the side, if desired.

Nutritional information: 319 calories, 28g protein, 4g carbohydrates, 22g fat, 0g fiber, 131mg cholesterol, 630mg sodium, 366mg potassium.

Wine Mussels

Yield: 2 servings | **Prep time:** 10 minutes | **Cook time:** 10 minutes

Ingredients:

- 1 pound fresh mussels, cleaned and debearded
- 2 tablespoons olive oil
- 2 cloves garlic, minced
- 1/4 cup white wine
- 1/4 cup chopped fresh parsley
- 1/4 cup chopped fresh cilantro
- 1/4 cup chopped fresh basil

Directions:

1. Preheat the air fryer to 400°F.
2. In a bowl, toss the cleaned mussels with olive oil and garlic.
3. Place the mussels in the air fryer basket and cook for 5 minutes.
4. Add the white wine to the mussels and cook for an additional 3-4 minutes until the mussels have opened.
5. Sprinkle the chopped herbs over the mussels and cook for an additional minute.
6. Serve hot.

Nutritional information: 239 calories, 16g protein, 4g carbohydrates, 17g fat, 0g fiber, 37mg cholesterol, 303mg sodium, 343mg potassium.

Honey Halibut

Yield: 2 servings | **Prep time:** 10 minutes | **Cook time:** 12 minutes

Ingredients:

- 2 halibut fillets (6 oz each)
- 2 tablespoons honey
- 1 tablespoon Dijon mustard
- 1 tablespoon olive oil
- 1 tablespoon fresh lemon juice
- 1 teaspoon smoked paprika
- 1/2 teaspoon garlic powder
- Salt and pepper, to taste

Directions:

1. Preheat the air fryer to 400°F (200°C).
2. In a small bowl, whisk together the honey, Dijon mustard, olive oil, lemon juice, smoked paprika, garlic powder, salt, and pepper until well combined.
3. Pat the halibut fillets dry with a paper towel and place them in the air fryer basket.
4. Brush the honey mustard mixture over the top of each halibut fillet.
5. Place the air fryer basket in the preheated air fryer and cook for 10-12 minutes, or until the halibut is cooked through and flakes easily with a fork.
6. Serve the halibut hot with your favorite sides.

Nutritional information: 296 calories, 36g protein, 15g carbohydrates, 10g fat, 0g fiber, 76mg cholesterol, 336mg sodium, 710mg potassium.

Oregano Swordfish

Yield: 2 servings | **Prep time:** 10 minutes | **Cook time:** 10 minutes

Ingredients:

- 2 swordfish steaks (6-8 ounces each)
- 2 tablespoons olive oil
- 1 teaspoon smoked paprika
- 1 teaspoon garlic powder
- 1 teaspoon dried oregano
- Salt and pepper, to taste
- Lemon wedges, for serving

Directions:

1. Preheat the air fryer to 400°F.
2. Rub the swordfish steaks with olive oil on both sides.
3. In a small bowl, mix together the smoked paprika, garlic powder, dried oregano, salt, and pepper.
4. Sprinkle the spice mixture evenly over both sides of the swordfish steaks.
5. Place the swordfish steaks in the air fryer basket and cook for 8-10 minutes or until the internal temperature reaches 145°F.
6. Serve with lemon wedges on the side.

Nutritional information: 331 calories, 39g protein, 2g carbohydrates, 18g fat, 1g fiber, 85mg cholesterol, 274mg sodium, 604mg potassium.

Sweet Salmon

Yield: 2 servings | **Prep time:** 10 minutes | **Cook time:** 15 minutes

Ingredients:

- 2 salmon fillets
- 1 mango, peeled and diced
- 1/2 red onion, diced
- 1/4 cup chopped fresh cilantro
- 1 tbsp olive oil
- 1 tbsp honey
- 1 tbsp lime juice
- 1 tsp paprika
- Salt and pepper to taste

Directions:

1. Preheat the air fryer to 390°F (200°C).
2. In a small bowl, whisk together the olive oil, honey, lime juice, paprika, salt, and pepper.
3. Place the salmon fillets in the air fryer basket and brush the tops with the honey-lime mixture.
4. Top the salmon with the diced mango and red onion.
5. Air fry for 12-15 minutes, until the salmon is cooked through and the mango and onion are slightly caramelized.
6. Remove the salmon from the air fryer and sprinkle with fresh cilantro before serving.

Nutritional information: 387 calories, 34g protein, 22g carbohydrates, 19g fat, 2g fiber, 93mg cholesterol, 107mg sodium, 984mg potassium.

Garlic Crab Cakes

Yield: 2 servings | **Prep time:** 15 minutes | **Cook time:** 15 minutes

Ingredients:

- 1/2 pound crabmeat
- 1/4 cup breadcrumbs
- 2 tablespoons mayonnaise
- 2 tablespoons finely chopped red onion
- 1 tablespoon dijon mustard
- 1 tablespoon lemon juice
- 1 tablespoon chopped fresh parsley
- 1/2 teaspoon garlic powder
- Salt and pepper, to taste

Directions:

1. In a medium bowl, mix together the crabmeat, breadcrumbs, mayonnaise, red onion, dijon mustard, lemon juice, parsley, garlic powder, salt, and pepper.
2. Form the mixture into 4-6 patties.
3. Preheat the air fryer to 375°F.
4. Spray the air fryer basket with cooking spray and place the crab cakes in the basket.
5. Cook for 12-15 minutes, or until the crab cakes are golden brown and cooked through, flipping halfway through cooking.
6. Serve with lemon wedges and tartar sauce, if desired.

Nutritional information: 188 calories, 18g protein, 8g carbohydrates, 10g fat, 0.5g fiber, 96mg cholesterol, 472mg sodium, 350mg potassium.

Hummus Wraps

Yield: 2 servings | **Prep time:** 15 minutes | **Cook time:** 10 minutes

Ingredients:

- 2 large flour tortillas
- 2 fillets of white fish (such as tilapia or cod), cut into strips
- 1/4 cup all-purpose flour
- 1 teaspoon paprika
- 1 teaspoon garlic powder
- Salt and pepper, to taste
- 1/4 cup hummus
- 1/4 cup tzatziki sauce
- 1 cup shredded lettuce
- 1/2 cup chopped tomato
- 1/4 cup chopped red onion
- 1/4 cup crumbled feta cheese

Directions:

1. Preheat your air fryer to 400°F (200°C).
2. In a shallow dish, mix together the flour, paprika, garlic powder, salt, and pepper.
3. Coat the fish strips in the flour mixture and place them in the air fryer basket.
4. Cook the fish in the air fryer for 8-10 minutes, flipping halfway through, until golden brown and crispy.
5. Warm the tortillas in the microwave for 10-15 seconds.
6. Spread a tablespoon of hummus and a tablespoon of tzatziki sauce onto each tortilla.
7. Top each tortilla with shredded lettuce, chopped tomato, chopped red onion, and crumbled feta cheese.
8. Add the cooked fish to each tortilla and wrap tightly.

Nutritional information: 545 calories, 37g protein, 56g carbohydrates, 17g fat, 5g fiber, 93mg cholesterol, 946mg sodium, 883mg potassium.

Poultry & Meat

Garlic Chicken

Yield: 2 servings | **Prep time:** 10 minutes | **Cook time:** 15 minutes

Ingredients:

- 2 boneless, skinless chicken breasts
- 1/4 cup basil pesto
- 1/4 cup breadcrumbs
- 1/4 cup grated parmesan cheese
- 1/2 teaspoon garlic powder
- Salt and pepper to taste

Directions:

1. Preheat the air fryer to 375°F (190°C).
2. Season the chicken breasts with salt, pepper, and garlic powder on both sides.
3. Spread a tablespoon of pesto on each chicken breast.
4. In a shallow dish, mix together the breadcrumbs and parmesan cheese.
5. Press the pesto-coated chicken breasts into the breadcrumb mixture, coating both sides.
6. Place the chicken breasts in the air fryer basket.
7. Air fry the chicken for 12-15 minutes, flipping halfway through, until the internal temperature reaches 165°F (74°C).
8. Serve hot with your favorite side dishes.

Nutritional information: 317 calories, 37g protein, 8g carbohydrates, 15g fat, 1g fiber, 92mg cholesterol, 533mg sodium, 414mg potassium.

Paprika Chicken Wings

Yield: 2 servings | **Prep time:** 10 minutes | **Cook time:** 25 minutes

Ingredients:

- 6 chicken wings
- 2 tablespoons olive oil
- 1 tablespoon honey
- 1 teaspoon paprika
- 1 teaspoon garlic powder
- 1/2 teaspoon dried oregano
- 1/4 teaspoon salt
- 1/4 teaspoon black pepper

Directions:

1. Preheat the air fryer to 400°F (200°C).
2. In a bowl, mix together olive oil, honey, paprika, garlic powder, dried oregano, salt, and black pepper.
3. Add chicken wings to the bowl and coat them with the mixture.
4. Place the chicken wings in the air fryer basket and cook for 10 minutes.
5. After 10 minutes, flip the chicken wings and cook for another 15 minutes.
6. Serve hot and enjoy!

Nutritional information: 362 calories, 20g protein, 10g carbohydrates, 27g fat, 0g fiber, 85mg cholesterol, 352mg sodium, 181mg potassium.

Oregano Chicken Drumsticks

Yield: 2 servings | **Prep time:** 10 minutes | **Cook time:** 20 minutes

Ingredients:

- 4 chicken drumsticks
- 2 tbsp olive oil
- 2 tsp paprika
- 1 tsp garlic powder
- 1 tsp dried oregano
- Salt and pepper to taste

Directions:

1. Preheat the air fryer to 400°F (200°C).
2. In a small bowl, mix together the olive oil, paprika, garlic powder, dried oregano, salt, and pepper.
3. Brush the mixture onto the chicken drumsticks, making sure to coat them evenly.
4. Place the drumsticks in the air fryer basket and cook for 10 minutes.
5. Flip the drumsticks over and cook for another 10 minutes or until they are golden brown and the internal temperature reaches 165°F (75°C).
6. Serve hot and enjoy!

Nutritional information: 300 calories, 28g protein, 2g carbohydrates, 20g fat, 1g fiber, 130mg cholesterol, 400mg sodium, 310mg potassium.

Tender Onion Chicken Breast

Yield: 2 servings | **Prep time:** 10 minutes | **Cook time:** 15 minutes

Ingredients:

- 2 boneless, skinless chicken breasts
- 1 tablespoon olive oil
- 1 tablespoon Cajun seasoning
- 1/2 teaspoon garlic powder
- 1/2 teaspoon onion powder
- 1/4 teaspoon salt
- 1/4 teaspoon black pepper

Directions:

1. Preheat the air fryer to 375°F (190°C).
2. Rub the chicken breasts with olive oil and sprinkle with Cajun seasoning, garlic powder, onion powder, salt, and black pepper on both sides.
3. Place the chicken breasts in the air fryer basket, making sure they don't overlap.
4. Cook for 12-15 minutes, flipping the chicken halfway through, until the internal temperature of the chicken reaches 165°F (74°C).
5. Let the chicken rest for 5 minutes before slicing and serving.

Nutritional information: 224 calories, 42g protein, 1g carbohydrates, 5g fat, 0g fiber, 99mg cholesterol, 453mg sodium, 401mg potassium.

Lemon and Garlic Beef Steak

Yield: 2 servings | **Prep time:** 5 minutes | **Cook time:** 10 minutes

Ingredients:

- 2 beef steaks, about 6 oz each
- 1 tbsp dried oregano
- 1 tbsp olive oil
- 1 tbsp lemon juice
- 2 garlic cloves, minced
- Salt and pepper to taste

Directions:

1. Preheat the air fryer to 400°F.
2. In a small bowl, mix together the oregano, olive oil, lemon juice, garlic, salt, and pepper.
3. Brush both sides of the beef steaks with the oregano mixture.
4. Place the steaks in the air fryer basket and cook for 8-10 minutes, flipping once halfway through.
5. Check the internal temperature of the steaks with a meat thermometer. For medium-rare, the temperature should be 135°F; for medium, it should be 145°F.
6. Remove the steaks from the air fryer and let them rest for a few minutes before serving.

Nutritional information: 310 calories, 43g protein, 1g carbohydrates, 14g fat, 1g fiber, 123mg cholesterol, 82mg sodium, 708mg potassium.

Spiced Beef Slices

Yield: 2 servings | **Prep time:** 10 minutes | **Cook time:** 10 minutes

Ingredients:

- 1 lb beef sirloin, sliced thinly
- 1 tsp smoked paprika
- 1 tsp garlic powder
- 1 tsp onion powder
- 1 tsp dried oregano
- 1/2 tsp salt
- 1/4 tsp black pepper
- 1 tbsp olive oil

Directions:

1. Preheat the air fryer to 400°F.
2. In a mixing bowl, combine the paprika, garlic powder, onion powder, oregano, salt, and black pepper.
3. Add the beef slices to the mixing bowl and coat them evenly with the spice mix.
4. Drizzle the olive oil over the beef slices and mix well.
5. Place the beef slices in the air fryer basket and cook for 8-10 minutes or until the beef is cooked to your liking.
6. Serve with your favorite Mediterranean sides such as rice, grilled vegetables, or a salad.

Nutritional information: 282 calories, 34g protein, 2g carbohydrates, 15g fat, 1g fiber, 104mg cholesterol, 496mg sodium, 539mg potassium.

Aromatic Chicken Thighs

Yield: 2 servings | **Prep time:** 10 minutes | **Cook time:** 20 minutes

Ingredients:

- 2 bone-in, skin-on chicken thighs
- 1 tablespoon olive oil
- 1 tablespoon lemon juice
- 1 teaspoon dried oregano
- 1/2 teaspoon garlic powder
- Salt and pepper to taste

Directions:

1. Preheat the air fryer to 375°F (190°C).
2. In a small bowl, mix together the olive oil, lemon juice, oregano, garlic powder, salt, and pepper.
3. Rub the mixture all over the chicken thighs, making sure to get under the skin.
4. Place the chicken thighs in the air fryer basket, skin-side down.
5. Cook for 10 minutes, then flip the chicken and cook for another 10-12 minutes, or until the internal temperature reaches 165°F (74°C) using a meat thermometer.
6. Let the chicken rest for a few minutes before serving.

Nutritional information: 261 calories, 20g protein, 1g carbohydrates, 19g fat, 0g fiber, 97mg cholesterol, 376mg sodium, 210mg potassium.

Fragrant Pork Steak

Yield: 2 servings | **Prep time:** 10 minutes | **Cook time:** 15 minutes

Ingredients:

- 2 pork steaks, about 8 oz each
- 2 tbsp olive oil
- 1 tsp dried thyme
- 1 tsp garlic powder
- 1/2 tsp salt
- 1/4 tsp black pepper

Directions:

1. Preheat the air fryer to 380°F.
2. In a small bowl, mix together the olive oil, thyme, garlic powder, salt, and black pepper.
3. Rub the spice mixture over the pork steaks, making sure to coat both sides.
4. Place the pork steaks in the air fryer basket and cook for 15 minutes, flipping them over halfway through.
5. Check the internal temperature of the pork steaks using a meat thermometer. They should reach an internal temperature of 145°F.
6. Let the pork steaks rest for 3-5 minutes before slicing and serving.

Nutritional information: 397 calories, 51g protein, 0g carbohydrates, 20g fat, 0g fiber, 165mg cholesterol, 750mg sodium, 590mg potassium.

Garlic Pork Loin

Yield: 2 servings | **Prep time:** 10 minutes | **Cook time:** 25 minutes

Ingredients:

- 1/2 lb. pork loin, sliced into 1-inch thick pieces
- 2 tbsp. olive oil
- 1 tbsp. dried sage
- 1 tsp. garlic powder
- 1/2 tsp. salt
- 1/4 tsp. black pepper

Directions:

1. Preheat the air fryer to 375°F.
2. In a small bowl, mix together the olive oil, dried sage, garlic powder, salt, and black pepper.
3. Brush both sides of the pork loin pieces with the oil mixture.
4. Place the pork in a single layer in the air fryer basket.
5. Cook for 20-25 minutes or until the pork is cooked through and the internal temperature reaches 145°F.
6. Let the pork rest for 5 minutes before serving.

Nutritional information: 277 calories, 31g protein, 1g carbohydrates, 16g fat, 0g fiber, 88mg cholesterol, 685mg sodium, 400mg potassium.

Sweet Lamb Ribs

Yield: 2 servings | **Prep time:** 10 minutes | **Cook time:** 20 minutes

Ingredients:

- 1 lb lamb ribs
- 2 tbsp honey
- 1 tbsp olive oil
- 2 garlic cloves, minced
- 1 tsp dried oregano
- 1/2 tsp paprika
- Salt and black pepper to taste

Directions:

1. Preheat the air fryer to 400°F.
2. In a small bowl, mix together honey, olive oil, minced garlic, dried oregano, paprika, salt, and black pepper.
3. Coat lamb ribs with the honey mixture and let marinate for 5 minutes.
4. Place the lamb ribs in the air fryer basket and cook for 10 minutes.
5. Flip the ribs and cook for an additional 10 minutes or until fully cooked.
6. Serve hot with your favorite sides.

Nutritional information: 563 calories, 29g protein, 14g carbohydrates, 44g fat, 0g fiber, 122mg cholesterol, 226mg sodium, 432mg potassium.

Tomatoes Meatballs

Yield: 2 servings | **Prep time:** 15 minutes | **Cook time:** 10 minutes

Ingredients:

- 1/2 pound ground beef
- 1/2 pound ground pork
- 1/2 cup breadcrumbs
- 1/4 cup chopped fresh basil
- 1/4 cup chopped sun-dried tomatoes
- 1 egg
- 1/2 teaspoon garlic powder
- Salt and pepper to taste
- Olive oil cooking spray

Directions:

1. In a mixing bowl, combine the ground beef, ground pork, breadcrumbs, chopped basil, chopped sun-dried tomatoes, egg, garlic powder, salt, and pepper. Mix well.
2. Form the mixture into 1-2 inch meatballs.
3. Preheat the air fryer to 375°F.
4. Lightly spray the air fryer basket with olive oil cooking spray.
5. Arrange the meatballs in a single layer in the air fryer basket.
6. Cook for 10 minutes, shaking the basket every 3-4 minutes to ensure even cooking.
7. Serve hot and enjoy!

Nutritional information: 370 calories, 32g protein, 17g carbohydrates, 19g fat, 1g fiber, 171mg cholesterol, 576mg sodium, 523mg potassium.

Lemon Lamb Cutlets

Yield: 2 servings | **Prep time:** 10 minutes | **Cook time:** 12 minutes

Ingredients:

- 4 lamb cutlets
- 2 tablespoons fresh dill, chopped
- 1 tablespoon olive oil
- 1 tablespoon lemon juice
- 1 teaspoon garlic powder
- Salt and black pepper to taste

Directions:

1. Preheat the air fryer to 400°F (200°C).
2. Season the lamb cutlets with salt, black pepper, and garlic powder on both sides.
3. In a small bowl, mix together the olive oil, lemon juice, and chopped dill.
4. Brush the lamb cutlets with the dill mixture on both sides.
5. Place the lamb cutlets in the air fryer basket and cook for 6 minutes.
6. Flip the lamb cutlets and cook for an additional 6 minutes, or until they are cooked to your desired level of doneness.
7. Serve the lamb cutlets hot, garnished with additional fresh dill, if desired.

Nutritional information: 294 calories, 33g protein, 1g carbohydrates, 17g fat, 0g fiber, 114mg cholesterol, 95mg sodium, 441mg potassium.

Tender Grilled Chicken

Yield: 2 servings | **Prep time:** 10 minutes | **Cook time:** 18 minutes

Ingredients:

- 2 chicken breasts, skinless and boneless
- 1 tbsp olive oil
- 2 tbsp fresh rosemary, chopped
- 2 garlic cloves, minced
- 1/2 tsp salt
- 1/4 tsp black pepper
- 1 lemon, cut into wedges

Directions:

1. Preheat the air fryer to 380°F (190°C).
2. In a small bowl, mix together the olive oil, rosemary, garlic, salt, and black pepper.
3. Rub the chicken breasts with the mixture on both sides.
4. Place the chicken breasts in the air fryer basket and cook for 15 minutes.
5. Flip the chicken breasts over and cook for another 3 minutes, or until the internal temperature of the chicken reaches 165°F (75°C).
6. Remove the chicken from the air fryer and let it rest for 5 minutes before slicing.
7. Serve with lemon wedges.

Nutritional information: 283 calories, 49g protein, 2g carbohydrates, 8g fat, 1g fiber, 145mg cholesterol, 655mg sodium, 634mg potassium.

Oregano Medallions

Yield: 2 servings | **Prep time:** 10 minutes | **Cook time:** 15 minutes

Ingredients:

- 2 beef tenderloin medallions (4-6 oz each)
- 1 tbsp olive oil
- 1 tsp dried oregano
- 1 tsp dried thyme
- 1/2 tsp garlic powder
- Salt and black pepper to taste

Directions:

1. Preheat the air fryer to 400°F.
2. Rub the beef tenderloin medallions with olive oil.
3. In a small bowl, mix together oregano, thyme, garlic powder, salt, and black pepper.
4. Rub the spice mixture onto the medallions, making sure to cover all sides.
5. Place the medallions in the air fryer basket and cook for 6-7 minutes per side, or until the internal temperature reaches 135°F for medium-rare, 145°F for medium, or 155°F for well done.
6. Remove the medallions from the air fryer and let them rest for 5 minutes before slicing and serving.

Nutritional information: 244 calories, 26g protein, 1g carbohydrates, 15g fat, 0g fiber, 89mg cholesterol, 106mg sodium, 359mg potassium.

Garlic Leg of Lamb

Yield: 2 servings | **Prep time:** 10 minutes | **Cook time:** 30 minutes

Ingredients:

- 1-pound boneless leg of lamb, cut into 1-inch thick slices
- 2 tablespoons chopped fresh mint
- 2 tablespoons olive oil
- 1 tablespoon lemon juice
- 1 teaspoon minced garlic
- Salt and pepper, to taste

Directions:

1. In a small bowl, mix together the mint, olive oil, lemon juice, garlic, salt, and pepper to make the marinade.
2. Place the lamb slices in a shallow dish and pour the marinade over them, making sure they are well coated. Cover and refrigerate for at least 1 hour, or up to 24 hours.
3. Preheat the air fryer to 400°F.
4. Place the marinated lamb slices in the air fryer basket in a single layer, leaving some space between them. Cook for 10-15 minutes, depending on the desired level of doneness and the thickness of the slices, flipping them halfway through cooking.
5. Once the lamb is cooked to your liking, remove it from the air fryer and let it rest for a few minutes before serving.

Nutritional information: 390 calories, 30g protein, 1g carbohydrates, 29g fat, 0g fiber, 126mg cholesterol, 128mg sodium, 401mg potassium.

Pepper Meat Mince

Yield: 2 servings | **Prep time:** 10 minutes | **Cook time:** 20 minutes

Ingredients:

- 1 lb ground beef
- 1 can (14.5 oz) diced tomatoes, drained
- 1/2 onion, chopped
- 1/2 red bell pepper, chopped
- 2 garlic cloves, minced
- 1 tsp dried oregano
- 1/2 tsp salt
- 1/4 tsp black pepper
- 1 tbsp olive oil

Directions:

1. In a bowl, combine the ground beef, diced tomatoes, onion, red bell pepper, garlic, oregano, salt, and black pepper. Mix well.
2. Grease the air fryer basket with olive oil.
3. Add the meat mixture to the basket and spread it evenly.
4. Air fry at 375°F for 20 minutes or until the meat is cooked through and the vegetables are tender.
5. Remove from the air fryer and serve hot.

Nutritional information: 445 calories, 39g protein, 12g carbohydrates, 28g fat, 3g fiber, 129mg cholesterol, 710mg sodium, 807mg potassium.

Onion Chorizo

Yield: 2 servings | **Prep time:** 10 minutes | **Cook time:** 15 minutes

Ingredients:

- 2 chorizo sausages, sliced
- 1 red bell pepper, sliced
- 1 yellow onion, sliced
- 1 tsp dried oregano
- 2 cloves garlic, minced
- 1 tbsp olive oil

Directions:

1. Preheat the air fryer to 375°F.
2. In a bowl, combine sliced chorizo, sliced bell pepper, sliced onion, minced garlic, dried oregano, and olive oil.
3. Toss to combine well and transfer to the air fryer basket.
4. Cook for 15 minutes or until the chorizo is crispy and the vegetables are tender.
5. Serve hot and enjoy!

Nutritional information: 425 calories, 21g protein, 12g carbohydrates, 34g fat, 3g fiber, 85mg cholesterol, 1350mg sodium, 570mg potassium.

Thyme Jerk Chicken

Yield: 2 servings | **Prep time:** 10 minutes | **Cook time:** 20 minutes

Ingredients:

- 2 boneless chicken breasts, cut into 1-inch pieces
- 1 tablespoon olive oil
- 1 tablespoon jerk seasoning
- 1 teaspoon dried thyme
- 1 teaspoon garlic powder
- 1 teaspoon onion powder
- Salt and black pepper to taste

Directions:

1. Preheat the air fryer to 375°F (190°C).
2. In a small bowl, combine the jerk seasoning, thyme, garlic powder, onion powder, salt, and black pepper.
3. In a separate bowl, toss the chicken pieces with olive oil to coat.
4. Sprinkle the seasoning mix over the chicken and toss to coat evenly.
5. Arrange the chicken in a single layer in the air fryer basket.
6. Air fry for 10 minutes, then flip the chicken pieces over and continue air frying for an additional 10 minutes or until the chicken is cooked through and the outside is crispy.
7. Serve hot with your favorite sides.

Nutritional information: 300 calories, 45g protein, 2g carbohydrates, 12g fat, 1g fiber, 130mg cholesterol, 500mg sodium, 600mg potassium.

Red Onion Chicken Skewers

Yield: 2 servings | **Prep time:** 15 minutes | **Cook time:** 15 minutes

Ingredients:

- 2 boneless, skinless chicken breasts, cut into cubes
- 1 red bell pepper, cut into chunks
- 1 yellow bell pepper, cut into chunks
- 1 red onion, cut into chunks
- 2 tablespoons olive oil
- 2 teaspoons dried oregano
- 1 teaspoon garlic powder
- Salt and pepper, to taste

Directions:

1. Preheat the air fryer to 400°F.
2. Thread the chicken, bell peppers, and onion onto skewers.
3. In a small bowl, whisk together the olive oil, oregano, garlic powder, salt, and pepper.
4. Brush the skewers with the olive oil mixture, making sure to coat all sides.
5. Place the skewers in the air fryer basket and cook for 15 minutes, flipping halfway through, or until the chicken is cooked through and the vegetables are tender.
6. Serve immediately.

Nutritional information: 309 calories, 30g protein, 12g carbohydrates, 16g fat, 3g fiber, 82mg cholesterol, 117mg sodium, 691mg potassium.

Parsley Chicken Patties

Yield: 2 servings | **Prep time:** 10 minutes | **Cook time:** 20 minutes

Ingredients:

- 1-pound ground chicken
- 1/2 cup panko breadcrumbs
- 1/4 cup chopped sun-dried tomatoes
- 1/4 cup chopped fresh parsley
- 1 tablespoon minced garlic
- 1 teaspoon dried oregano
- Salt and pepper, to taste
- Cooking spray

Directions:

1. Preheat the air fryer to 375°F.
2. In a large bowl, combine the ground chicken, panko breadcrumbs, sun-dried tomatoes, parsley, garlic, oregano, salt, and pepper.
3. Mix until well combined.
4. Divide the mixture into 4 equal portions and shape into patties.
5. Spray the air fryer basket with cooking spray.
6. Place the chicken patties in the basket, making sure they are not touching.
7. Cook for 10 minutes, then flip the patties and cook for another 10 minutes, or until the internal temperature reaches 165°F.
8. Serve hot with your favorite Mediterranean sides.

Nutritional information: 285 calories, 28g protein, 12g carbohydrates, 14g fat, 1g fiber, 105mg cholesterol, 382mg sodium, 471mg potassium.

Vegetables

Greek Style Kalamata Olives

Yield: 2 servings | **Prep time:** 5 minutes | **Cook time:** 8 minutes

Ingredients:

- 1 cup Kalamata olives, drained
- 1 tablespoon extra-virgin olive oil
- 1 teaspoon dried oregano
- 1 teaspoon minced garlic
- 1/2 teaspoon red pepper flakes
- 1/4 teaspoon black pepper

Directions:

1. In a mixing bowl, combine the Kalamata olives, olive oil, dried oregano, minced garlic, red pepper flakes, and black pepper. Toss well to coat the olives evenly.
2. Preheat your air fryer to 400°F (200°C).
3. Once the air fryer is preheated, place the seasoned olives in the air fryer basket in a single layer.
4. Air fry the olives at 400°F (200°C) for 8 minutes, shaking the basket halfway through to ensure even cooking.
5. Remove the olives from the air fryer and let them cool for a few minutes before serving.

Nutritional information: 140 calories, 1g protein, 3g carbohydrates, 14g fat, 1g fiber, 0mg cholesterol, 540mg sodium, 15mg potassium

Tender Asparagus

Yield: 2 servings | **Prep time:** 10 minutes | **Cook time:** 8 minutes

Ingredients:

- 1 bunch of asparagus, trimmed
- 2 tablespoons olive oil
- 2 tablespoons grated Parmesan cheese
- 1 teaspoon garlic powder
- 1/2 teaspoon salt
- 1/4 teaspoon black pepper
- Fresh lemon wedges for serving (optional)

Directions:

1. Preheat your air fryer to 400°F (200°C).
2. In a large mixing bowl, toss the trimmed asparagus with olive oil, Parmesan cheese, garlic powder, salt, and black pepper until well coated.
3. Place the seasoned asparagus in a single layer in the air fryer basket.
4. Air fry the asparagus at 400°F (200°C) for 8 minutes, or until they are tender and crispy, shaking the basket halfway through cooking to ensure even cooking.
5. Remove the asparagus from the air fryer and transfer them to a serving plate.
6. Serve hot with fresh lemon wedges for an extra burst of flavor, if desired.

Nutritional information: 120 calories, 5g protein, 6g carbohydrates, 9g fat, 3g fiber, 5mg cholesterol, 250mg sodium, 480mg potassium

Paprika Okra

Yield: 2 servings | **Prep time:** 10 minutes | **Cook time:** 12 minutes

Ingredients:

- 1 cup fresh okra, trimmed and halved lengthwise
- 2 cloves garlic, minced
- 2 tablespoons olive oil
- 1 teaspoon dried oregano
- 1/2 teaspoon smoked paprika
- 1/2 teaspoon salt
- 1/4 teaspoon black pepper
- Lemon wedges, for serving

Directions:

1. In a mixing bowl, toss the okra with minced garlic, olive oil, dried oregano, smoked paprika, salt, and black pepper until evenly coated.
2. Preheat the air fryer to 375°F (190°C) for 5 minutes.
3. Place the seasoned okra in the air fryer basket in a single layer.
4. Air fry the okra at 375°F (190°C) for 10-12 minutes, shaking the basket halfway through, until the okra is crispy and golden brown.
5. Remove the okra from the air fryer and transfer to a serving plate.
6. Serve hot with lemon wedges for added freshness.

Nutritional information: 150 calories, 2g protein, 10g carbohydrates, 12g fat, 4g fiber, 0mg cholesterol, 300mg sodium, 500mg potassium

Paprika Corn

Yield: 2 servings | **Prep time:** 10 minutes | **Cook time:** 12 minutes

Ingredients:

- 2 ears of corn, husked and halved
- 1 tablespoon olive oil
- 1 teaspoon paprika
- 1/2 teaspoon garlic powder
- 1/2 teaspoon dried oregano
- 1/2 teaspoon dried thyme
- Salt and pepper to taste
- 2 tablespoons grated parmesan cheese
- Fresh parsley, chopped (optional)

Directions:

1. Preheat your air fryer to 400°F (200°C).
2. In a bowl, toss the corn halves with olive oil, paprika, garlic powder, dried oregano, dried thyme, salt, and pepper until evenly coated.
3. Place the corn halves in a single layer in the air fryer basket.
4. Air fry for 12 minutes, turning halfway through, or until the corn is golden brown and crispy.
5. Sprinkle grated parmesan cheese over the cooked corn and air fry for an additional 1-2 minutes until the cheese is melted and bubbly.
6. Remove the corn from the air fryer and sprinkle with fresh parsley, if desired.
7. Serve hot and enjoy!

Nutritional information: 180 calories, 5g protein, 22g carbohydrates, 10g fat, 3g fiber, 5mg cholesterol, 180mg sodium, 365mg potassium

Thyme Beets

Yield: 2 servings | **Prep time:** 10 minutes | **Cook time:** 15 minutes

Ingredients:

- 2 medium-sized beets, peeled and thinly sliced
- 1 tablespoon olive oil
- 1/4 teaspoon garlic powder
- 1/4 teaspoon dried thyme
- 1/4 teaspoon dried oregano
- 1/4 teaspoon salt
- 1/4 teaspoon black pepper
- 1/2 cup shredded mozzarella cheese
- 2 tablespoons grated parmesan cheese

Directions:

1. Preheat your air fryer to 400°F (200°C) for 5 minutes.
2. In a large mixing bowl, toss the sliced beets with olive oil, garlic powder, dried thyme, dried oregano, salt, and black pepper until well coated.
3. Place the seasoned beet slices in a single layer in the air fryer basket.
4. Air fry the beets at 400°F (200°C) for 10 minutes, flipping halfway through the cooking time.
5. After 10 minutes, sprinkle the shredded mozzarella cheese and grated parmesan cheese evenly over the beet slices.
6. Continue air frying for an additional 5 minutes, or until the cheese is melted and the beets are crispy on the edges.
7. Remove the air fryer basket carefully and let the cheesy beets cool for a few minutes before serving.

Nutritional information: 192 calories, 9g protein, 12g carbohydrates, 13g fat, 3g fiber, 23mg cholesterol, 388mg sodium, 439mg potassium

Paprika Broccoli

Yield: 2 servings | **Prep time:** 10 minutes | **Cook time:** 12 minutes

Ingredients:

- 1 small head of broccoli, cut into florets
- 2 tablespoons olive oil
- 2 teaspoons chili powder
- 1/2 teaspoon garlic powder
- 1/2 teaspoon onion powder
- 1/2 teaspoon paprika
- 1/4 teaspoon cumin
- 1/4 teaspoon salt
- 1/4 teaspoon black pepper

Directions:

1. In a large mixing bowl, combine olive oil, chili powder, garlic powder, onion powder, paprika, cumin, salt, and black pepper. Stir well to make a marinade.
2. Add the broccoli florets to the marinade and toss until evenly coated.
3. Preheat your air fryer to 400°F (200°C) for 5 minutes.
4. Place the marinated broccoli florets in the air fryer basket in a single layer.
5. Air fry at 400°F (200°C) for 12 minutes, shaking the basket halfway through to ensure even cooking.
6. Once done, remove the broccoli from the air fryer and serve hot.

Nutritional information: 112 calories, 3g protein, 11g carbohydrates, 7g fat, 4g fiber, 0mg cholesterol, 254mg sodium, 487mg potassium

Garlic Cauliflower Florets

Yield: 2 servings | **Prep time:** 10 minutes | **Cook time:** 12 minutes

Ingredients:

- 1 small head of cauliflower, cut into florets
- 2 tablespoons olive oil
- 2 tablespoons chopped fresh mint
- 1 tablespoon lemon juice
- 1 teaspoon minced garlic
- 1/2 teaspoon salt
- 1/4 teaspoon black pepper
- Optional: Lemon wedges, for serving
- Optional: Fresh mint leaves, for garnish

Directions:

1. In a large mixing bowl, toss the cauliflower florets with olive oil, chopped mint, lemon juice, minced garlic, salt, and black pepper until well coated.
2. Preheat your air fryer to 375°F (190°C) for 5 minutes.
3. Place the seasoned cauliflower florets in the air fryer basket in a single layer, making sure they are not too crowded.
4. Air fry the cauliflower florets at 375°F (190°C) for 10-12 minutes, shaking the basket halfway through to ensure even cooking, until the florets are tender and lightly browned.
5. Remove the cauliflower florets from the air fryer and transfer to a serving dish.
6. Serve hot with lemon wedges and garnish with fresh mint leaves, if desired.

Nutritional information: 142 calories, 3g protein, 10g carbohydrates, 11g fat, 4g fiber, 0mg cholesterol, 369mg sodium, 476mg potassium

Lemon Artichoke

Yield: 2 servings | **Prep time:** 10 minutes | **Cook time:** 12 minutes

Ingredients:

- 2 large artichokes, trimmed and halved
- 2 tablespoons olive oil
- 2 cloves garlic, minced
- 1 tablespoon chopped fresh basil
- 1/2 teaspoon salt
- 1/4 teaspoon black pepper
- 1 tablespoon lemon juice
- 2 tablespoons grated Parmesan cheese
- Lemon wedges, for serving

Directions:

1. In a bowl, combine olive oil, minced garlic, chopped basil, salt, and black pepper. Stir well to make a marinade.
2. Brush the artichoke halves with the marinade, making sure to coat all sides.
3. Preheat your air fryer to 375°F (190°C).
4. Place the artichoke halves in the air fryer basket, cut side down, in a single layer.
5. Cook in the air fryer for 12 minutes, or until the artichokes are tender and lightly browned, flipping them halfway through cooking.

6. Remove the artichokes from the air fryer and drizzle them with lemon juice. Sprinkle with grated Parmesan cheese.
7. Serve hot with lemon wedges for squeezing over the top.

Nutritional information: 180 calories, 6g protein, 17g carbohydrates, 11g fat, 8g fiber, 3mg cholesterol, 440mg sodium, 590mg potassium

Cinnamon Carrots

Yield: 2 servings | **Prep time:** 10 minutes | **Cook time**: 12 minutes

Ingredients:

- 4 large carrots, peeled and cut into thin sticks
- 2 tablespoons olive oil
- 1 teaspoon ground cumin
- 1/2 teaspoon ground paprika
- 1/2 teaspoon ground turmeric
- 1/4 teaspoon ground cinnamon
- Salt and pepper to taste
- Fresh parsley for garnish (optional)

Directions:

1. In a large mixing bowl, toss the carrot sticks with olive oil, ground cumin, paprika, turmeric, cinnamon, salt, and pepper until well coated.
2. Preheat your air fryer to 400°F (200°C) for 3-5 minutes.
3. Place the seasoned carrot sticks in a single layer in the air fryer basket, making sure they are not overcrowded.
4. Air fry the carrots at 400°F (200°C) for 10-12 minutes, shaking the basket halfway through to ensure even cooking, until the carrots are tender and slightly crispy on the edges.
5. Remove the carrots from the air fryer and let them cool for a minute.
6. Transfer the air-fried cumin carrots to a serving plate and garnish with fresh parsley, if desired.

Nutritional information: 120 calories, 1g protein, 12g carbohydrates, 8g fat, 3g fiber, 0mg cholesterol, 180mg sodium, 460mg potassium.

Onion Potatoes

Yield: 2 servings | **Prep time:** 10 minutes | **Cook time**: 25 minutes

Ingredients:

- 2 large potatoes, washed and cut into cubes
- 1 tablespoon olive oil
- 1 teaspoon dried oregano
- 1/2 teaspoon garlic powder
- 1/2 teaspoon onion powder
- 1/4 teaspoon salt
- 1/4 teaspoon black pepper
- Fresh parsley, chopped (optional for garnish)

Directions:

1. In a large mixing bowl, toss the cubed potatoes with olive oil, dried oregano, garlic powder, onion powder, salt, and black pepper until well coated.
2. Preheat your air fryer to 400°F (200°C).

3. Place the seasoned potato cubes in the air fryer basket in a single layer, making sure they are not touching each other.
4. Cook the potatoes in the air fryer for 20-25 minutes, shaking the basket halfway through, until they are golden brown and crispy.
5. Once cooked, carefully remove the potatoes from the air fryer and transfer them to a serving dish.
6. Garnish with fresh chopped parsley, if desired, and serve hot.

Nutritional information: 180 calories, 3g protein, 31g carbohydrates, 5g fat, 3g fiber, 0mg cholesterol, 150mg sodium, 770mg potassium.

Oregano Snap Peas

Yield: 2 servings | **Prep time:** 5 minutes | **Cook time:** 8 minutes

Ingredients:

- 2 cups snap peas, ends trimmed
- 1 tablespoon olive oil
- 1 tablespoon lemon juice
- 1 teaspoon lemon zest
- 1/2 teaspoon salt
- 1/4 teaspoon black pepper
- 1/4 teaspoon garlic powder
- 1/4 teaspoon dried oregano
- Lemon slices for garnish (optional)

Directions:

1. In a medium bowl, toss the snap peas with olive oil, lemon juice, lemon zest, salt, black pepper, garlic powder, and dried oregano until evenly coated.
2. Preheat your air fryer to 400°F (200°C) for 5 minutes.
3. Place the seasoned snap peas in the air fryer basket in a single layer, making sure they are not overlapping.
4. Cook the snap peas in the air fryer for 8 minutes, shaking the basket halfway through to ensure even cooking.
5. Once the snap peas are crispy and tender, remove them from the air fryer and transfer to a serving dish.
6. Garnish with lemon slices, if desired.
7. Serve hot and enjoy!

Nutritional information: 100 calories, 2g protein, 10g carbohydrates, 7g fat, 3g fiber, 0mg cholesterol, 240mg sodium, 300mg potassium

Cumin Butternut Squash

Yield: 2 servings | **Prep time:** 15 minutes | **Cook time:** 20 minutes

Ingredients:

- 1 cup canned chickpeas, drained and rinsed
- 1 cup diced butternut squash
- 1 tablespoon olive oil
- 1 teaspoon paprika
- 1/2 teaspoon ground cumin
- 1/2 teaspoon garlic powder
- 1/4 teaspoon salt
- 1/4 teaspoon black pepper

- Fresh parsley, chopped, for garnish (optional)

Directions:

1. In a mixing bowl, combine the chickpeas, diced butternut squash, olive oil, paprika, ground cumin, garlic powder, salt, and black pepper. Toss to coat the chickpeas and butternut squash in the seasoning mixture.
2. Preheat your air fryer to 375°F (190°C).
3. Place the seasoned chickpeas and butternut squash in the air fryer basket in a single layer.
4. Air fry for 18-20 minutes, shaking the basket halfway through to ensure even cooking, until the chickpeas and butternut squash are crispy and golden brown.
5. Remove from the air fryer and let cool for a few minutes. Garnish with chopped fresh parsley, if desired.
6. Serve as a side dish, on top of a salad, or as a tasty snack.

Nutritional information: 235 calories, 9g protein, 35g carbohydrates, 7g fat, 9g fiber, 0mg cholesterol, 354mg sodium, 745mg potassium

Honey Apple Wedges

Yield: 2 servings | **Prep time:** 10 minutes | **Cook time**: 12 minutes

Ingredients:

- 2 medium apples, cored and cut into wedges
- 1 tablespoon olive oil
- 1 tablespoon honey
- 1/2 teaspoon ground cinnamon
- 1/4 teaspoon ground nutmeg
- Pinch of salt
- Optional: Chopped nuts (such as walnuts or almonds) for garnish
- Optional: Greek yogurt or vanilla ice cream for serving

Directions:

1. Preheat your air fryer to 350°F (175°C) for 5 minutes.
2. In a medium bowl, whisk together the olive oil, honey, ground cinnamon, ground nutmeg, and a pinch of salt.
3. Add the apple wedges to the bowl and toss to coat them evenly with the honey mixture.
4. Place the coated apple wedges in a single layer in the air fryer basket.
5. Bake in the air fryer at 350°F (175°C) for 12 minutes or until the apples are tender and lightly golden, shaking the basket once or twice during cooking to ensure even cooking.
6. Remove the apple wedges from the air fryer and let them cool slightly.
7. Optional: Garnish with chopped nuts, if desired.
8. Serve warm as a delicious and healthy dessert on their own or with a dollop of Greek yogurt or a scoop of vanilla ice cream for added indulgence.

Nutritional information: 120 calories, 0.5g protein, 28g carbohydrates, 3g fat, 3g fiber, 0mg cholesterol, 15mg sodium, 195mg potassium

Oregano Zucchini Sticks

Yield: 2 servings | **Prep time:** 15 minutes | **Cook time:** 10 minutes

Ingredients:

- 1 medium zucchini, cut into sticks
- 1/2 cup all-purpose flour
- 2 large eggs, beaten
- 1 cup bread crumbs
- 1/2 cup grated Parmesan cheese
- 1 tsp dried oregano
- 1 tsp dried basil
- Salt and pepper to taste
- Olive oil cooking spray

Directions:

1. Preheat your air fryer to 400°F (200°C) for 5 minutes.
2. In a shallow dish, place the flour. In another shallow dish, beat the eggs. In a third shallow dish, combine bread crumbs, Parmesan cheese, dried oregano, dried basil, salt, and pepper.
3. Coat each zucchini stick with flour, then dip in beaten eggs, and coat with the breadcrumb mixture, pressing gently to adhere.
4. Spray the air fryer basket with olive oil cooking spray. Place the coated zucchini sticks in a single layer in the air fryer basket.
5. Spray the coated zucchini sticks with olive oil cooking spray.
6. Air fry at 400°F (200°C) for 10 minutes, flipping halfway through, until golden and crispy.
7. Remove from the air fryer and serve hot with your favorite dipping sauce.

Nutritional information: 258 calories, 15g protein, 26g carbohydrates, 10g fat, 2g fiber, 123mg cholesterol, 563mg sodium, 381mg potassium

Garlic Mushroom Caps

Yield: 2 servings | **Prep time:** 10 minutes | **Cook time:** 12 minutes

Ingredients:

- 4 large mushroom caps
- 2 tablespoons olive oil
- 2 cloves garlic, minced
- 1/2 teaspoon dried oregano
- 1/2 teaspoon dried thyme
- 1/4 teaspoon salt
- 1/4 teaspoon black pepper
- 1/4 cup crumbled feta cheese
- 2 tablespoons chopped fresh parsley

Directions:

1. Preheat your air fryer to 375°F (190°C).
2. Clean the mushroom caps and remove the stems.
3. In a small bowl, whisk together olive oil, minced garlic, dried oregano, dried thyme, salt, and black pepper.
4. Brush the mushroom caps with the olive oil mixture, coating both sides.
5. Place the mushroom caps in the air fryer basket, gill side up.
6. Air fry for 10 minutes.

7. After 10 minutes, remove the mushroom caps from the air fryer, sprinkle with crumbled feta cheese, and return them to the air fryer for an additional 2 minutes, until the cheese is melted and slightly golden.
8. Remove the mushroom caps from the air fryer and sprinkle with chopped fresh parsley before serving.

Nutritional information: 148 calories, 5g protein, 6g carbohydrates, 12g fat, 2g fiber, 17mg cholesterol, 335mg sodium, 441mg potassium

Thyme Eggplant

Yield: 2 servings | **Prep time:** 10 minutes | **Cook time:** 12 minutes

Ingredients:

- 1 medium eggplant, sliced into 1/2-inch rounds
- 2 tablespoons olive oil
- 2 cloves garlic, minced
- 1/2 teaspoon dried oregano
- 1/2 teaspoon dried thyme
- 1/4 teaspoon salt
- 1/4 teaspoon black pepper
- Fresh parsley for garnish

Directions:

1. Preheat your air fryer to 400°F (200°C) for 5 minutes.
2. In a small bowl, combine olive oil, minced garlic, dried oregano, dried thyme, salt, and black pepper.
3. Brush both sides of the eggplant slices with the olive oil mixture.
4. Place the eggplant slices in a single layer in the air fryer basket, making sure they do not overlap.
5. Air fry the eggplant slices at 400°F (200°C) for 6 minutes, then flip the slices and air fry for an additional 6 minutes, or until they are golden brown and tender.
6. Remove the air fryer basket and let the eggplant slices cool for a few minutes.
7. Garnish with fresh parsley before serving.

Nutritional information: 137 calories, 2g protein, 12g carbohydrates, 10g fat, 5g fiber, 0mg cholesterol, 151mg sodium, 388mg potassium

Feta Beets

Yield: 2 servings | **Prep time:** 10 minutes | **Cook time:** 20 minutes

Ingredients:

- 2 medium beets, peeled and cut into 1-inch cubes
- 1 tablespoon olive oil
- 1 teaspoon dried oregano
- 1/2 teaspoon salt
- 1/4 teaspoon black pepper
- 1/4 cup crumbled feta cheese
- 2 tablespoons chopped fresh parsley

Directions:

1. Preheat the air fryer to 400°F (200°C).

2. In a bowl, toss the beet cubes with olive oil, dried oregano, salt, and black pepper until well coated.
3. Place the seasoned beet cubes in the air fryer basket in a single layer.
4. Air fry the beets for 18-20 minutes, shaking the basket halfway through, until they are tender and lightly browned.
5. Remove the roasted beets from the air fryer and transfer them to a serving dish.
6. Sprinkle crumbled feta cheese and chopped fresh parsley over the roasted beets.
7. Serve hot as a side dish or a salad topping.

Nutritional information: 180 calories, 5g protein, 16g carbohydrates, 11g fat, 4g fiber, 17mg cholesterol, 528mg sodium, 607mg potassium

Thyme Cabbage

Yield: 2 servings | **Prep time:** 10 minutes | **Cook time:** 20 minutes

Ingredients:

- 1 small head of cabbage, thinly sliced
- 2 tablespoons olive oil
- 2 cloves garlic, minced
- 1 teaspoon dried oregano
- 1 teaspoon dried thyme
- 1 teaspoon smoked paprika
- Salt and pepper, to taste
- 1/4 cup vegetable broth
- 2 tablespoons chopped fresh parsley, for garnish (optional)

Directions:

1. Preheat the air fryer to 375°F (190°C).
2. In a large bowl, toss the thinly sliced cabbage with olive oil, minced garlic, dried oregano, dried thyme, smoked paprika, salt, and pepper.
3. Place the seasoned cabbage in the air fryer basket in a single layer.
4. Pour vegetable broth over the cabbage.
5. Air fry for 15-20 minutes, stirring halfway through, until the cabbage is tender and lightly browned.
6. Remove from the air fryer and transfer to a serving dish.
7. Garnish with chopped fresh parsley, if desired.

Nutritional information: 130 calories, 3g protein, 18g carbohydrates, 6g fat, 6g fiber, 0mg cholesterol, 310mg sodium, 470mg potassium

Garlic Carrots

Yield: 2 servings | **Prep time:** 10 minutes | **Cook time:** 15 minutes

Ingredients:

- 1 lb carrots, peeled and cut into evenly-sized sticks
- 2 tbsp olive oil
- 1 tbsp fresh rosemary, minced
- 2 cloves garlic, minced
- 1/2 tsp salt
- 1/4 tsp black pepper
- 1 tbsp balsamic vinegar
- 1 tbsp honey
- Optional: Fresh parsley for garnish

Directions:

1. In a large bowl, toss the carrot sticks with olive oil, minced rosemary, minced garlic, salt, and black pepper until well-coated.
2. Preheat your air fryer to 375°F (190°C).
3. Place the seasoned carrot sticks in the air fryer basket in a single layer, making sure they are not overcrowded.
4. Air fry the carrots for 12-15 minutes, shaking the basket halfway through cooking, until the carrots are tender and lightly browned.
5. In a small bowl, whisk together balsamic vinegar and honey.
6. Once the carrots are cooked, drizzle the balsamic honey mixture over the top and toss to coat evenly.
7. Cook for an additional 2-3 minutes to caramelize the glaze slightly.
8. Remove the carrots from the air fryer and let them cool slightly.
9. Garnish with fresh parsley, if desired, and serve hot.

Nutritional information: 150 calories, 2g protein, 20g carbohydrates, 7g fat, 4g fiber, 0mg cholesterol, 400mg sodium, 650mg potassium

Cumin Avocado Cubes

Yield: 2 servings | **Prep time:** 10 minutes | **Cook time:** 8 minutes

Ingredients:

- 1 ripe avocado, peeled, pitted, and cut into cubes
- 2 cloves garlic, minced
- 1 tablespoon olive oil
- 1/2 teaspoon paprika
- 1/2 teaspoon cumin
- 1/4 teaspoon salt
- 1/4 teaspoon black pepper
- Fresh cilantro, chopped (optional, for garnish)

Directions:

- In a medium bowl, combine minced garlic, olive oil, paprika, cumin, salt, and black pepper. Stir well to make a marinade.
- Add the avocado cubes to the marinade and gently toss to coat them evenly.
- Preheat your air fryer to 375°F (190°C) for 5 minutes.
- Place the marinated avocado cubes in a single layer in the air fryer basket.
- Air fry the avocado cubes at 375°F (190°C) for 8 minutes, flipping them halfway through the cooking time to ensure even browning.
- Once cooked, remove the avocado cubes from the air fryer and let them cool for a few minutes.
- Garnish with chopped cilantro, if desired, and serve hot.

Nutritional information: 196 calories, 2g protein, 9g carbohydrates, 18g fat, 7g fiber, 0mg cholesterol, 150mg sodium, 487mg potassium.

Bread and Pizza

Cherry Tomatoes Pizza

Yield: 2 servings | **Prep time:** 15 minutes | **Cook time:** 10 minutes

Ingredients:

- 2 Portobello mushroom caps
- 1/4 cup pizza sauce
- 1/4 cup shredded mozzarella cheese
- 1/4 cup sliced cherry tomatoes
- 1/4 cup sliced black olives
- 1/4 cup chopped fresh spinach
- Salt and pepper to taste

Directions:

1. Preheat the air fryer to 375°F (190°C).
2. Remove the stems from the mushroom caps and use a spoon to gently scrape out the gills.
3. Season the mushroom caps with salt and pepper.
4. Spread pizza sauce over each mushroom cap.
5. Top each mushroom cap with shredded mozzarella cheese, sliced cherry tomatoes, black olives, and chopped spinach.
6. Place the mushroom caps in the air fryer basket and cook for 10 minutes or until the cheese is melted and bubbly.
7. Serve hot and enjoy!

Nutritional information: 123 calories, 9g protein, 7g carbohydrates, 7g fat, 3g fiber, 13mg cholesterol, 342mg sodium, 553mg potassium.

Hummus Flatbread

Yield: 2 servings | **Prep time:** 10 minutes | **Cook time:** 10 minutes

Ingredients:

- 2 pieces of whole wheat flatbread
- 6 oz. turkey breast, sliced
- 1/4 cup hummus
- 1/2 cup diced tomatoes
- 1/4 cup chopped Kalamata olives
- 1/4 cup crumbled feta cheese
- 1 tbsp. chopped fresh parsley

Directions:

1. Preheat the air fryer to 400°F.
2. Spread hummus evenly over each flatbread.
3. Top each flatbread with turkey slices, diced tomatoes, Kalamata olives, and feta cheese.
4. Place flatbreads in the air fryer and cook for 8-10 minutes, until crispy.
5. Sprinkle fresh parsley over the top of each flatbread.
6. Serve hot.

Nutritional information: 420 calories, 38g protein, 41g carbohydrates, 12g fat, 7g fiber, 85mg cholesterol, 1040mg sodium, 630mg potassium.

Blueberries Pizza

Yield: 2 servings | **Prep time:** 10 minutes | **Cook time:** 8 minutes

Ingredients:

- 2 pieces of whole wheat flatbread
- 2 tablespoons of honey
- 1/2 cup of sliced strawberries
- 1/2 cup of blueberries
- 1/4 cup of crumbled feta cheese
- 1/4 cup of chopped fresh mint
- Cooking spray

Directions:

1. Preheat the air fryer to 360°F.
2. Spray the air fryer basket with cooking spray.
3. Place the flatbread in the air fryer basket and cook for 4 minutes.
4. Remove the flatbread from the air fryer and drizzle each with 1 tablespoon of honey.
5. Top each flatbread with the sliced strawberries, blueberries, and crumbled feta cheese.
6. Return the flatbreads to the air fryer and cook for an additional 4 minutes, until the cheese is melted and the fruit is heated through.
7. Garnish with chopped fresh mint and serve.

Nutritional information: 327 calories, 10g protein, 59g carbohydrates, 7g fat, 7g fiber, 16mg cholesterol, 322mg sodium, 510mg potassium.

Basil Pinwheels

Yield: 4 servings | **Prep time:** 15 minutes | **Cook time:** 10 minutes

Ingredients:

- 1 sheet puff pastry
- 1/4 cup grated Parmesan cheese
- 1/4 cup grated mozzarella cheese
- 1/4 cup ricotta cheese
- 1/4 cup chopped fresh basil
- 1 egg, beaten
- Salt and pepper to taste

Directions:

1. Preheat the air fryer to 400°F.
2. Roll out the puff pastry on a floured surface to a rectangle shape.
3. In a bowl, mix together Parmesan, mozzarella, ricotta, and basil.
4. Spread the cheese mixture over the puff pastry, leaving a 1/2 inch border.
5. Roll up the puff pastry, starting with the long end, to form a log.
6. Brush the beaten egg over the log and season with salt and pepper.
7. Cut the log into 1-inch slices.
8. Place the slices in the air fryer basket, making sure to leave space between each slice.
9. Air fry for 8-10 minutes until golden brown and crispy.
10. Serve warm.

Nutritional information: 305 calories, 10g protein, 17g carbohydrates, 21g fat, 1g fiber, 56mg cholesterol, 409mg sodium, 127mg potassium.

Walnuts Bread

Yield: 8 servings | **Prep time:** 10 minutes | **Cook time:** 20 minutes

Ingredients:

- 1 cup all-purpose flour
- 1/2 cup whole wheat flour
- 1/2 cup dried cranberries
- 1/4 cup chopped walnuts
- 1/2 teaspoon baking powder
- 1/2 teaspoon baking soda
- 1/4 teaspoon salt
- 1/2 cup plain Greek yogurt
- 1/4 cup honey
- 1 egg
- 2 tablespoons olive oil
- 1 teaspoon vanilla extract

Directions:

1. Preheat the air fryer to 350°F.
2. In a medium bowl, combine the all-purpose flour, whole wheat flour, dried cranberries, chopped walnuts, baking powder, baking soda, and salt.
3. In a separate bowl, whisk together the Greek yogurt, honey, egg, olive oil, and vanilla extract.
4. Add the wet ingredients to the dry ingredients and mix until just combined.
5. Pour the batter into a greased air fryer-safe loaf pan.
6. Place the pan in the air fryer basket and cook for 20 minutes, or until a toothpick inserted in the center comes out clean.
7. Let the bread cool in the pan for 5 minutes before removing and slicing.

Nutritional information: 205 calories, 5g protein, 33g carbohydrates, 6g fat, 2g fiber, 27mg cholesterol, 199mg sodium, 112mg potassium.

Cheese Flatbread

Yield: 2 servings | **Prep time:** 10 minutes | **Cook time:** 10 minutes

Ingredients:

- 2 whole wheat flatbreads
- 2 tbsp. tomato sauce
- 1/2 cup shredded mozzarella cheese
- 1/4 cup sliced Kalamata olives
- 1/4 cup sliced red onion
- 1/4 cup chopped fresh spinach

Directions:

1. Preheat the air fryer to 360°F.
2. Spread 1 tbsp. of tomato sauce over each flatbread.
3. Sprinkle shredded mozzarella cheese evenly over the flatbreads.
4. Top the cheese with sliced olives, red onion, and chopped spinach.
5. Place the flatbreads in the air fryer and cook for 10 minutes or until the cheese is melted and bubbly.
6. Remove the flatbreads from the air fryer and slice into pieces. Serve hot.

Nutritional information: 330 calories, 18g protein, 39g carbohydrates, 11g fat, 7g fiber, 22mg cholesterol, 780mg sodium, 350mg potassium.

Mozzarella Tart

Yield: 2 servings | **Prep time:** 15 minutes | **Cook time:** 10 minutes

Ingredients:

- 1 sheet frozen puff pastry, thawed
- 1 large ripe tomato, sliced
- 4 oz fresh mozzarella cheese, sliced
- 1/4 cup fresh basil leaves
- 1 tbsp extra-virgin olive oil
- 1 tbsp balsamic vinegar
- Salt and pepper to taste

Directions:

1. Preheat the air fryer to 375°F (190°C).
2. Roll out the puff pastry sheet on a floured surface and cut it into two squares.
3. Place the puff pastry squares on the air fryer basket and prick them with a fork.
4. Air fry for 5 minutes until they are puffed and golden.
5. Remove the basket from the air fryer and top the puff pastry squares with tomato slices, mozzarella slices, and basil leaves.
6. Drizzle the tart with olive oil and balsamic vinegar.
7. Season with salt and pepper to taste.
8. Air fry for an additional 5 minutes until the cheese is melted and bubbly.
9. Serve warm.

Nutritional information: 483 calories, 13g protein, 36g carbohydrates, 32g fat, 1g fiber, 41mg cholesterol, 453mg sodium, 384mg potassium.

Honey Bread

Yield: 4 servings | **Prep time:** 15 minutes | **Cook time:** 20 minutes

Ingredients:

- 1 cup all-purpose flour
- 1/2 cup grated carrots
- 1/4 cup honey
- 1/4 cup plain Greek yogurt
- 1/4 cup olive oil
- 1 tsp baking powder
- 1/2 tsp baking soda
- 1/2 tsp cinnamon
- 1/4 tsp salt

Directions:

1. Preheat air fryer to 325°F (165°C).
2. In a medium bowl, whisk together the flour, baking powder, baking soda, cinnamon, and salt.
3. In another bowl, mix together the grated carrots, honey, Greek yogurt, and olive oil.
4. Add the wet mixture to the dry mixture and stir until just combined.
5. Grease a small loaf pan with olive oil and pour in the batter.
6. Place the pan in the air fryer basket and cook for 20 minutes or until a toothpick inserted into the center comes out clean.
7. Remove the pan from the air fryer and let cool for 5 minutes before slicing and serving.

Nutritional information: 300 calories, 4g protein, 42g carbohydrates, 14g fat, 2g fiber, 0mg cholesterol, 330mg sodium, 135mg potassium.

Olives Pizza

Yield: 2 servings | **Prep time:** 10 minutes | **Cook time:** 10 minutes

Ingredients:

- 2 whole wheat naan bread
- 1/2 cup tomato sauce
- 1/2 tsp dried oregano
- 1/4 tsp garlic powder
- 1/2 cup shredded mozzarella cheese
- 1/4 cup sliced pepperoni
- 1/4 cup sliced black olives
- Fresh basil leaves, chopped (optional)

Directions:

1. Preheat the air fryer to 350°F (175°C).
2. Spread 1/4 cup of tomato sauce on each naan bread, leaving about 1/2 inch border around the edges.
3. Sprinkle oregano and garlic powder over the tomato sauce.
4. Add shredded mozzarella cheese on top of the sauce, followed by pepperoni and black olives.
5. Place the prepared naan bread in the air fryer basket and cook for 10 minutes, or until the cheese is melted and bubbly.
6. Once done, remove the pizza from the air fryer and let it cool for a few minutes.
7. Sprinkle chopped fresh basil leaves (optional) over the pizza and serve.

Nutritional information: 485 calories, 25g protein, 52g carbohydrates, 20g fat, 9g fiber, 47mg cholesterol, 1000mg sodium, 510mg potassium.

Feta Pizza

Yield: 2 servings | **Prep time:** 10 minutes | **Cook time:** 12 minutes

Ingredients:

- 1 pre-made pizza crust
- 1/4 cup marinara sauce
- 1/2 cup shredded mozzarella cheese
- 1/2 cup canned artichoke hearts, drained and chopped
- 1/4 cup sliced kalamata olives
- 1/4 cup crumbled feta cheese
- 1 tablespoon chopped fresh parsley

Directions:

1. Preheat the air fryer to 380°F (190°C) for 5 minutes.
2. Place the pizza crust in the air fryer basket and cook for 4 minutes.
3. Remove the pizza crust from the air fryer and spread the marinara sauce on top.
4. Sprinkle the shredded mozzarella cheese over the sauce.
5. Top with the chopped artichoke hearts and sliced kalamata olives.
6. Return the pizza to the air fryer basket and cook for an additional 6-8 minutes or until the cheese is melted and the crust is crispy.
7. Sprinkle the crumbled feta cheese and chopped parsley over the pizza before serving.

Nutritional information: 536 calories, 27g protein, 56g carbohydrates, 23g fat, 7g fiber, 40mg cholesterol, 1638mg sodium, 430mg potassium.

Tender Pizza

Yield: 2 servings | **Prep time:** 10 minutes | **Cook time:** 10 minutes

Ingredients:

- 1 pre-made pizza crust
- 1/4 cup tomato sauce
- 1/2 cup shredded mozzarella cheese
- 1/4 cup crumbled feta cheese
- 1/4 cup shredded Parmesan cheese
- 1/4 cup shredded provolone cheese
- 1/4 cup sliced black olives
- 1/4 cup sliced sun-dried tomatoes
- 1/4 cup chopped fresh basil

Directions:

1. Preheat the air fryer to 375°F (190°C).
2. Place the pre-made pizza crust on a cutting board or other flat surface. Spread the tomato sauce evenly over the crust.
3. Sprinkle the shredded mozzarella cheese over the tomato sauce, followed by the crumbled feta cheese, shredded Parmesan cheese, and shredded provolone cheese.
4. Add the sliced black olives and sun-dried tomatoes on top of the cheese.
5. Place the pizza in the air fryer basket and cook for 10 minutes, or until the crust is golden brown and the cheese is melted and bubbly.
6. Carefully remove the pizza from the air fryer using tongs or a spatula. Sprinkle with chopped fresh basil before serving.

Nutritional information: 559 calories, 32g protein, 50g carbohydrates, 26g fat, 4g fiber, 74mg cholesterol, 1523mg sodium, 396mg potassium.

Yogurt Bread

Yield: 6 servings | **Prep time:** 10 minutes | **Cook time:** 30 minutes

Ingredients:

- 1 cup all-purpose flour
- 1/2 cup granulated sugar
- 1/2 teaspoon baking powder
- 1/2 teaspoon baking soda
- 1/4 teaspoon salt
- 1/2 cup plain Greek yogurt
- 1/4 cup olive oil
- 1 large egg
- 1 lemon, zested and juiced

Directions:

1. Preheat the air fryer to 320°F (160°C).
2. In a large bowl, whisk together the flour, sugar, baking powder, baking soda, and salt.
3. In another bowl, whisk together the yogurt, olive oil, egg, lemon zest, and lemon juice until smooth.
4. Pour the wet ingredients into the dry ingredients and stir until just combined.
5. Pour the batter into a greased 6-inch loaf pan and place it in the air fryer basket.
6. Air fry for 25-30 minutes, or until a toothpick inserted into the center of the bread comes out clean.

7. Remove the bread from the air fryer and allow it to cool for a few minutes before slicing and serving.

Nutritional information: 229 calories, 5g protein, 35g carbohydrates, 8g fat, 1g fiber, 33mg cholesterol, 202mg sodium, 64mg potassium.

Plain Bread

Yield: 8 pita breads | **Prep time:** 15 minutes | **Cook time:** 8 minutes

Ingredients:

- 2 cups all-purpose flour
- 1 tsp salt
- 1 tbsp sugar
- 1 tbsp active dry yeast
- 1/4 cup warm water
- 3/4 cup warm milk
- 2 tbsp olive oil
- 1 egg, beaten

Directions:

1. In a large mixing bowl, combine flour, salt, and sugar.
2. In a small bowl, dissolve yeast in warm water and let it sit for 5 minutes until foamy.
3. Add the yeast mixture, warm milk, olive oil, and beaten egg to the dry ingredients. Mix until a soft dough forms.
4. Knead the dough on a lightly floured surface for about 5 minutes until smooth and elastic.
5. Place the dough in a greased bowl and cover with a damp towel. Let it rise in a warm place for 1 hour.
6. Preheat the air fryer to 375°F (190°C).
7. Punch down the dough and divide it into 8 pieces. Roll each piece into a ball and then flatten into a disk about 1/4 inch thick.
8. Place the disks in the air fryer basket in a single layer. Cook for 4 minutes, then flip and cook for another 4 minutes or until golden brown.
9. Remove from the air fryer and let cool for a few minutes before serving.

Nutritional information: 158 calories, 4g protein, 25g carbohydrates, 4g fat, 1g fiber, 15mg cholesterol, 316mg sodium, 72mg potassium.

Basil Pizza

Yield: 2 servings | **Prep time:** 10 minutes | **Cook time:** 10 minutes

Ingredients:

- 2 whole wheat pitas
- 1/2 cup marinara sauce
- 4 oz fresh mozzarella, sliced
- 1/4 cup chopped fresh basil
- 1/4 tsp garlic powder
- 1/4 tsp dried oregano
- Salt and pepper to taste
- Cooking spray

Directions:

1. Preheat air fryer to 375°F.
2. Spread 1/4 cup marinara sauce over each pita, leaving a small border around the edge.

3. Arrange mozzarella slices over the sauce.
4. Sprinkle chopped basil, garlic powder, dried oregano, salt, and pepper over the mozzarella.
5. Place the pizzas in the air fryer basket and spray with cooking spray.
6. Air fry for 8-10 minutes, or until the cheese is melted and the crust is crispy.
7. Carefully remove the pizzas from the air fryer and let cool for a few minutes before slicing and serving.

Nutritional information: 371 calories, 21g protein, 45g carbohydrates, 12g fat, 8g fiber, 31mg cholesterol, 801mg sodium, 286mg potassium.

Garlic Bread

Yield: 4 servings | **Prep time:** 10 minutes | **Cook time:** 15 minutes

Ingredients:

- 2 cups all-purpose flour
- 2 teaspoons baking powder
- 1/2 teaspoon salt
- 1/2 teaspoon garlic powder
- 1/2 teaspoon dried oregano
- 1/2 teaspoon dried basil
- 3/4 cup plain Greek yogurt
- 1/4 cup crumbled feta cheese
- 1/4 cup chopped black olives

Directions:

1. In a large mixing bowl, combine the flour, baking powder, salt, garlic powder, oregano, and basil. Stir well to combine.
2. Add the Greek yogurt, feta cheese, and black olives to the dry ingredients. Stir until the mixture comes together into a ball of dough.
3. Knead the dough on a lightly floured surface for a minute or two until it becomes smooth and elastic.
4. Divide the dough into 4 equal portions and shape each one into a flat disk.
5. Preheat the air fryer to 350°F (175°C).
6. Place the flat disks of dough into the air fryer basket, making sure they don't touch each other.
7. Air fry for 12-15 minutes, until the bread is golden brown and cooked through.
8. Serve warm or at room temperature.

Nutritional information: Calories: 266 | Protein: 12g | Carbohydrates: 42g | Fat: 5g | Fiber: 2g | Cholesterol: 13mg | Sodium: 569mg | Potassium: 168mg

Pasta

Greens Pasta

Yield: 2 servings | **Prep time:** 10 minutes | **Cook time:** 15 minutes

Ingredients:

- 6 oz. penne pasta
- 2 boneless, skinless chicken breasts, cubed
- 2 cups baby spinach
- 1/2 cup sun-dried tomatoes, chopped
- 2 cloves garlic, minced
- 1/4 cup feta cheese, crumbled
- Salt and pepper, to taste

Directions:

1. Preheat the air fryer to 400°F.
2. Cook pasta according to package instructions and set aside.
3. Season the chicken with salt and pepper and add to the air fryer basket. Cook for 6-8 minutes, flipping halfway through.
4. Add minced garlic to the air fryer basket and cook for an additional minute.
5. Remove the chicken and garlic from the air fryer and add them to the pot with cooked pasta.
6. Add the baby spinach and sun-dried tomatoes to the air fryer basket and cook for 1-2 minutes until spinach is wilted.
7. Add the spinach and sun-dried tomatoes to the pot with chicken and pasta and mix everything together.
8. Top with crumbled feta cheese and serve.

Nutritional information: 519 calories, 45g protein, 58g carbohydrates, 11g fat, 6g fiber, 116mg cholesterol, 456mg sodium, 1067mg potassium.

Tender Ravioli with Olives

Yield: 2 servings | **Prep time:** 10 minutes | **Cook time:** 15 minutes

Ingredients:

- 9 oz. cheese ravioli
- 1/4 cup chopped artichoke hearts
- 1/4 cup sliced Kalamata olives
- 2 tbsp olive oil
- 1 tsp dried oregano
- Salt and pepper to taste
- Grated Parmesan cheese for serving

Directions:

1. Preheat the air fryer to 400°F.
2. In a mixing bowl, combine the cheese ravioli, chopped artichoke hearts, sliced Kalamata olives, olive oil, dried oregano, salt, and pepper. Toss well to combine.
3. Transfer the mixture to the air fryer basket and cook for 15 minutes, shaking the basket occasionally to ensure even cooking.
4. Once cooked, remove from the air fryer and serve with grated Parmesan cheese.

Nutritional information: 510 calories, 20g protein, 51g carbohydrates, 25g fat, 6g fiber, 30mg cholesterol, 1000mg sodium, 370mg potassium.

Oregano Pasta

Yield: 2 servings | **Prep time:** 5 minutes | **Cook time**: 10 minutes

Ingredients:

- 8 oz. spaghetti
- 2 tbsp. olive oil
- 4 garlic cloves, minced
- 2 medium-sized tomatoes, diced
- 1/4 tsp. dried oregano
- 1/4 tsp. dried basil
- Salt and pepper to taste

Directions:

1. Preheat the air fryer to 400°F.
2. Cook spaghetti according to package instructions, drain and set aside.
3. In a mixing bowl, toss diced tomatoes with olive oil, minced garlic, dried oregano, dried basil, salt, and pepper.
4. Spread the tomato mixture in the air fryer basket and air fry for 5 minutes.
5. Add the cooked spaghetti to the air fryer basket, and toss with the tomato mixture.
6. Air fry for an additional 5 minutes, stirring halfway through.
7. Serve hot and enjoy!

Nutritional information: 393 calories, 10g protein, 59g carbohydrates, 13g fat, 4g fiber, 0mg cholesterol, 6mg sodium, 665mg potassium.

Fish Pasta

Yield: 2 servings | **Prep time:** 10 minutes | **Cook time**: 20 minutes

Ingredients:

- 8 oz salmon fillet
- 4 oz whole wheat spaghetti
- 1/4 cup prepared pesto
- 1/2 cup cherry tomatoes, halved
- 1/4 cup sliced black olives
- 1/4 cup crumbled feta cheese
- Salt and pepper, to taste

Directions:

1. Preheat the air fryer to 375°F.
2. Season the salmon fillet with salt and pepper and place it in the air fryer basket. Air fry for 10-12 minutes, or until the salmon is cooked through and flakes easily with a fork.
3. While the salmon is cooking, cook the spaghetti according to the package instructions until al dente. Drain and set aside.
4. In a large bowl, mix together the cooked spaghetti, pesto, cherry tomatoes, black olives, and feta cheese.
5. Divide the pasta between two serving bowls and top each with a cooked salmon fillet. Serve immediately.

Nutritional information: 555 calories, 39g protein, 38g carbohydrates, 28g fat, 5g fiber, 70mg cholesterol, 573mg sodium, 829mg potassium.

Mushrooms and Oregano Pasta

Yield: 2 servings | **Prep time:** 10 minutes | **Cook time:** 20 minutes

Ingredients:

- 6 oz spaghetti
- 1 cup Brussels sprouts, halved
- 1 cup mushrooms, sliced
- 2 cloves garlic, minced
- 2 tbsp olive oil
- 1 tsp dried oregano
- Salt and pepper, to taste
- Grated Parmesan cheese, for serving

Directions:

1. Preheat the air fryer to 400°F.
2. Cook spaghetti according to package instructions and set aside.
3. In a bowl, mix together Brussels sprouts, mushrooms, garlic, olive oil, dried oregano, salt, and pepper until well coated.
4. Place the vegetables in the air fryer basket and cook for 10-12 minutes, shaking the basket halfway through.
5. Add the cooked spaghetti to the air fryer basket and cook for an additional 2-3 minutes, until heated through and slightly crispy.
6. Divide the pasta into bowls, sprinkle with Parmesan cheese, and serve.

Nutritional information: 390 calories, 12g protein, 50g carbohydrates, 16g fat, 8g fiber, 3mg cholesterol, 58mg sodium, 800mg potassium.

Aromatic Ravioli with Tomatoes

Yield: 2 servings | **Prep time:** 10 minutes | **Cook time:** 12 minutes

Ingredients:

- 9 oz. cheese ravioli
- 1 cup cherry tomatoes, halved
- 2 cups baby spinach
- 2 cloves garlic, minced
- 1 tbsp olive oil
- 1/4 tsp salt
- 1/4 tsp black pepper
- 1/4 tsp red pepper flakes
- 2 tbsp grated Parmesan cheese

Directions:

1. Preheat air fryer to 375°F (190°C).
2. In a large bowl, combine the ravioli, cherry tomatoes, baby spinach, minced garlic, olive oil, salt, black pepper, and red pepper flakes. Toss to coat.
3. Transfer the mixture to the air fryer basket and cook for 10-12 minutes, shaking the basket halfway through cooking.
4. Once the ravioli is crispy and the tomatoes have softened, remove from the air fryer and divide the mixture between two plates.
5. Sprinkle grated Parmesan cheese over the top of each plate and serve.

Nutritional information: 430 calories, 18g protein, 46g carbohydrates, 20g fat, 4g fiber, 44mg cholesterol, 814mg sodium, 449mg potassium.

Spaghetti & Parsley Meatballs

Yield: 2 servings | **Prep time:** 15 minutes | **Cook time:** 20 minutes

Ingredients:

- 8 oz spaghetti
- 1 lb ground chicken
- 1/4 cup breadcrumbs
- 1 egg
- 1/4 cup chopped parsley
- 1/4 cup grated Parmesan cheese
- 1 tsp garlic powder
- Salt and pepper to taste
- 1/2 cup marinara sauce

Directions:

1. Cook spaghetti according to package instructions and set aside.
2. In a mixing bowl, combine ground chicken, breadcrumbs, egg, parsley, Parmesan cheese, garlic powder, salt, and pepper. Mix well.
3. Using your hands, form the mixture into 1-inch meatballs.
4. Preheat the air fryer to 375°F.
5. Place the meatballs in the air fryer basket, making sure they are not touching. Cook for 10 minutes.
6. Flip the meatballs and cook for another 5-7 minutes, until cooked through.
7. In a separate saucepan, heat the marinara sauce over medium heat.
8. Add the cooked spaghetti and meatballs to the saucepan and toss until coated with sauce.
9. Serve hot and enjoy!

Nutritional information: 570 calories, 45g protein, 50g carbohydrates, 21g fat, 3g fiber, 270mg cholesterol, 860mg sodium, 700mg potassium.

Parmesan Pasta

Yield: 2 servings | **Prep time:** 10 minutes | **Cook time:** 10 minutes

Ingredients:

- 6 oz spaghetti
- 1/4 cup olive oil
- 4 garlic cloves, minced
- 1/2 tsp red pepper flakes
- 1 lemon, zested and juiced
- 1/4 cup grated Parmesan cheese
- 1/4 cup chopped fresh parsley
- Salt and black pepper to taste

Directions:

1. Cook spaghetti according to package directions until al dente, then drain and set aside.
2. In a small bowl, whisk together olive oil, minced garlic, red pepper flakes, lemon zest, and lemon juice.
3. Preheat air fryer to 400°F.
4. Place cooked spaghetti in the air fryer basket and toss with the lemon garlic sauce.
5. Cook in the air fryer for 5 minutes, shaking the basket every minute or so to ensure even cooking.
6. After 5 minutes, remove the basket and sprinkle the pasta with Parmesan cheese, fresh parsley, salt, and black pepper. Toss to combine.

7. Return the basket to the air fryer and cook for an additional 2-3 minutes, until the cheese is melted and the pasta is lightly browned and crispy.
8. Serve hot and enjoy!

Nutritional information: 468 calories, 12g protein, 57g carbohydrates, 21g fat, 3g fiber, 8mg cholesterol, 142mg sodium, 191mg potassium.

Tender Pasta with Olives

Yield: 2 servings | **Prep time:** 10 minutes | **Cook time:** 15 minutes

Ingredients:

- 6 oz. spaghetti
- 1 cup asparagus, chopped
- 1/2 cup cherry tomatoes, halved
- 1/4 cup Kalamata olives, pitted and chopped
- 2 cloves garlic, minced
- 2 tbsp olive oil
- Salt and pepper to taste
- 2 tbsp grated Parmesan cheese

Directions:

1. Cook spaghetti according to package instructions until al dente. Drain and set aside.
2. In a mixing bowl, toss together chopped asparagus, cherry tomatoes, Kalamata olives, minced garlic, and olive oil. Season with salt and pepper.
3. Preheat the air fryer to 375°F (190°C).
4. Transfer the vegetable mixture to the air fryer basket and cook for 10 minutes, shaking the basket once or twice during cooking.
5. Add the cooked spaghetti to the air fryer basket and cook for an additional 5 minutes, tossing the mixture occasionally.
6. Serve hot, topped with grated Parmesan cheese.

Nutritional information: 462 calories, 13g protein, 55g carbohydrates, 21g fat, 6g fiber, 4mg cholesterol, 337mg sodium, 531mg potassium.

Italian Style Pasta

Yield: 2 servings | **Prep time:** 10 minutes | **Cook time:** 20 minutes

Ingredients:

- 4 ounces uncooked pasta
- 2 Italian sausages, casings removed and crumbled
- 1 tablespoon olive oil
- 2 cups chopped kale
- 1/4 cup chopped sun-dried tomatoes
- 2 cloves garlic, minced
- 1/2 teaspoon dried oregano
- Salt and black pepper to taste
- 1/4 cup grated Parmesan cheese

Directions:

1. Cook pasta according to package instructions until al dente.
2. Meanwhile, preheat the air fryer to 400°F.
3. In a mixing bowl, combine crumbled Italian sausage, olive oil, chopped kale, sun-dried tomatoes, minced garlic, dried oregano, salt, and black pepper.

4. Toss to combine well and transfer the mixture to the air fryer basket.
5. Cook for 10 minutes, stirring occasionally, until the sausage is browned and the kale is crispy.
6. Drain the cooked pasta and reserve 1/4 cup of pasta water.
7. Add the cooked pasta to the air fryer basket and toss to combine with the sausage and kale mixture.
8. If the pasta seems dry, add reserved pasta water to the air fryer and toss again.
9. Cook for another 3-5 minutes until the pasta is warmed through.
10. Serve with grated Parmesan cheese.

Nutritional information: 538 calories, 26g protein, 45g carbohydrates, 28g fat, 3g fiber, 65mg cholesterol, 1076mg sodium, 586mg potassium.

Seafood Pasta

Yield: 2 servings | **Prep time:** 10 minutes | **Cook time:** 20 minutes

Ingredients:

- 6 oz pasta
- 4 oz salmon, cut into chunks
- 6 oz shrimp, peeled and deveined
- 1/2 cup cherry tomatoes, halved
- 1/2 cup sliced red onion
- 2 cloves garlic, minced
- 1/4 cup chopped fresh parsley
- 1/4 cup crumbled feta cheese
- 2 tbsp olive oil
- Salt and pepper to taste

Directions:

1. Preheat the air fryer to 400°F.
2. Cook the pasta according to package instructions until al dente. Drain and set aside.
3. In a bowl, toss the salmon and shrimp with olive oil, garlic, salt, and pepper.
4. Spread the salmon, shrimp, cherry tomatoes, and red onion in a single layer in the air fryer basket. Air fry for 8-10 minutes or until the salmon and shrimp are cooked through.
5. In a large bowl, combine the cooked pasta, air fried salmon and shrimp mixture, chopped parsley, and feta cheese. Toss well to combine.
6. Divide the pasta mixture between two plates and serve immediately.

Nutritional information: 549 calories, 42g protein, 52g carbohydrates, 20g fat, 4g fiber, 155mg cholesterol, 547mg sodium, 882mg potassium.

Zucchini and Pasta

Yield: 2 servings | **Prep time:** 10 minutes | **Cook time:** 15 minutes

Ingredients:

- 6 oz. penne pasta
- 1 red bell pepper, sliced
- 1 yellow squash, sliced
- 1 zucchini, sliced
- 1/2 red onion, sliced
- 2 tbsp. olive oil
- 1 tsp. dried oregano
- Salt and black pepper, to taste
- 1/4 cup crumbled feta cheese (optional)

Directions:

1. Cook the penne pasta according to package instructions until al dente. Drain and set aside.
2. Preheat the air fryer to 400°F.
3. In a large bowl, combine the sliced red bell pepper, yellow squash, zucchini, and red onion. Drizzle with olive oil and season with dried oregano, salt, and black pepper.
4. Place the seasoned vegetables in the air fryer basket in a single layer. Cook for 12-15 minutes or until the vegetables are tender and lightly browned, tossing them halfway through the cooking time.
5. In a large serving bowl, combine the cooked penne pasta and roasted vegetables. Toss to combine.
6. Sprinkle with crumbled feta cheese, if desired.
7. Serve warm and enjoy!

Nutritional information: 439 calories, 12g protein, 63g carbohydrates, 17g fat, 7g fiber, 0mg cholesterol, 127mg sodium, 1283mg potassium.

Basil Pasta

Yield: 2 servings | **Prep time:** 10 minutes | **Cook time**: 20 minutes

Ingredients:

- 8 oz spaghetti
- 2 tbsp olive oil
- 2 cloves garlic, minced
- 1/4 tsp red pepper flakes
- 1 can (14.5 oz) diced tomatoes, drained
- 1/4 cup chopped fresh basil
- Salt and pepper to taste
- 1/4 cup crumbled feta cheese

Directions:

1. Cook spaghetti according to package directions until al dente.
2. While spaghetti is cooking, heat olive oil in a large skillet over medium-high heat. Add garlic and red pepper flakes and cook for 1 minute, stirring constantly.
3. Add drained tomatoes and cook for 5-7 minutes, stirring occasionally, until the tomatoes start to break down and form a sauce.
4. Add chopped basil and season with salt and pepper to taste. Reduce heat to low and simmer for 5 minutes.
5. Once spaghetti is cooked, drain and add to the tomato sauce. Toss to coat evenly.
6. Serve with crumbled feta cheese on top.

Nutritional information: 536 calories, 17g protein, 68g carbohydrates, 22g fat, 5g fiber, 17mg cholesterol, 360mg sodium, 780mg potassium.

Marinara Pasta

Yield: 2 servings | **Prep time:** 10 minutes | **Cook time:** 20 minutes

Ingredients:

- 6 oz penne pasta
- 2 boneless, skinless chicken breasts, cut into cubes
- 1/4 cup all-purpose flour
- 1/4 cup breadcrumbs
- 1/4 cup grated Parmesan cheese
- 1 tsp dried basil
- 1/2 tsp garlic powder
- Salt and pepper, to taste
- 1/2 cup marinara sauce
- 1/2 cup shredded mozzarella cheese

Directions:

1. Cook the penne pasta according to package instructions, then drain and set aside.
2. In a shallow dish, mix together the flour, breadcrumbs, Parmesan cheese, basil, garlic powder, salt, and pepper.
3. Dip each chicken cube into the mixture, making sure it's fully coated, then place it into the air fryer basket.
4. Air fry the chicken cubes at 380°F for 8-10 minutes, flipping halfway through.
5. Once the chicken is cooked through, remove it from the air fryer basket and set aside.
6. Pour the marinara sauce over the cooked pasta and stir to combine.
7. Divide the pasta between two plates, then top with the cooked chicken cubes and shredded mozzarella cheese.
8. Place the plates in the air fryer and air fry at 380°F for 2-3 minutes, or until the cheese is melted and bubbly.
9. Serve hot and enjoy!

Nutritional information: 574 calories, 45g protein, 59g carbohydrates, 16g fat, 3g fiber, 107mg cholesterol, 852mg sodium, 670mg potassium.

Olives and Pasta

Yield: 2 servings | **Prep time:** 10 minutes | **Cook time:** 20 minutes

Ingredients:

- 6 oz fusilli pasta
- 1/2 lb chicken breast, cut into small pieces
- 1 tbsp olive oil
- 1/2 red onion, diced
- 1/2 cup cherry tomatoes, halved
- 1/2 cup Kalamata olives, pitted and sliced
- 1/4 cup crumbled feta cheese
- 1/4 cup chopped fresh parsley
- Salt and pepper, to taste

Directions:

1. Cook the pasta according to package instructions until al dente. Drain and set aside.
2. In a bowl, toss the chicken with olive oil and season with salt and pepper.
3. Preheat the air fryer to 400°F. Once heated, add the chicken to the basket and cook for 8-10 minutes, flipping halfway through.

4. In a large pan over medium heat, sauté the red onion until softened.
5. Add the cherry tomatoes and cook until they start to burst.
6. Add the cooked pasta, olives, and cooked chicken to the pan, stirring to combine.
7. Top with crumbled feta cheese and chopped parsley.
8. Serve hot.

Nutritional information: 496 calories, 38g protein, 50g carbohydrates, 15g fat, 6g fiber, 87mg cholesterol, 949mg sodium, 697mg potassium.

Rice and Grains

Mussels Paella

Yield: 2 servings | **Prep time:** 20 minutes | **Cook time:** 20 minutes

Ingredients:

- 1/2 cup Arborio rice
- 1 cup chicken broth
- 1/2 teaspoon paprika
- 1/4 teaspoon saffron threads
- 1/4 teaspoon salt
- 1/4 teaspoon black pepper
- 4-5 large shrimp, peeled and deveined
- 4-5 small clams, cleaned
- 4-5 mussels, cleaned
- 1/2 cup diced tomatoes
- 1/4 cup diced onion
- 1/4 cup chopped bell pepper
- 1 tablespoon olive oil
- 1 tablespoon chopped fresh parsley

Directions:

1. In a large bowl, mix together the rice, chicken broth, paprika, saffron, salt, and black pepper.
2. Place the shrimp, clams, and mussels on top of the rice mixture.
3. Add the diced tomatoes, onion, and bell pepper on top of the seafood.
4. Drizzle the olive oil over the top of everything.
5. Place the mixture in the air fryer basket and cook at 375°F for 20 minutes.
6. Once done, let the paella cool for a few minutes before serving. Garnish with fresh parsley.

Nutritional information: 374 calories, 26g protein, 45g carbohydrates, 9g fat, 1g fiber, 80mg cholesterol, 938mg sodium, 478mg potassium.

Green Rice

Yield: 2 servings | **Prep time:** 5 minutes | **Cook time:** 20 minutes

Ingredients:

- 1 cup white rice
- 1 3/4 cups water
- 2 tablespoons pesto sauce
- 1/4 teaspoon salt
- 1/8 teaspoon black pepper
- 1/4 cup chopped sun-dried tomatoes
- 1/4 cup chopped Kalamata olives
- 2 tablespoons crumbled feta cheese

Directions:

1. Rinse the rice in cold water and drain well.
2. Add the rice, water, pesto sauce, salt, and black pepper to the air fryer basket and mix well.
3. Set the air fryer to 350°F and cook for 20 minutes.
4. Once done, open the air fryer and fluff the rice with a fork.
5. Add in the chopped sun-dried tomatoes and Kalamata olives and stir well.
6. Sprinkle the crumbled feta cheese on top and serve.

Nutritional information: 335 calories, 7g protein, 49g carbohydrates, 11g fat, 3g fiber, 8mg cholesterol, 515mg sodium, 238mg potassium.

Eggplant Rice

Yield: 2 servings | **Prep time:** 10 minutes | **Cook time:** 20 minutes

Ingredients:

- 1 cup uncooked basmati rice
- 1 1/2 cups water
- 1/2 cup diced bell pepper
- 1/2 cup diced zucchini
- 1/2 cup diced eggplant
- 1/2 cup cherry tomatoes, halved
- 1 tablespoon olive oil
- 1/2 teaspoon dried oregano
- Salt and pepper to taste

Directions:

1. Rinse the rice in a fine-mesh strainer under cold water until the water runs clear.
2. In a bowl, mix together the rice, water, olive oil, and dried oregano.
3. Add the diced vegetables to the rice mixture and stir to combine.
4. Pour the mixture into the air fryer basket and spread it out evenly.
5. Cook at 350°F for 20 minutes, or until the rice is cooked and the vegetables are tender.
6. Season with salt and pepper to taste.
7. Serve hot and enjoy!

Nutritional information: 324 calories, 6g protein, 53g carbohydrates, 10g fat, 4g fiber, 0mg cholesterol, 10mg sodium, 621mg potassium.

Garlic Rice

Yield: 2 servings | **Prep time:** 10 minutes | **Cook time:** 20 minutes

Ingredients:

- 1 cup basmati rice
- 1 1/2 cups water
- 1/2 cup canned diced tomatoes, drained
- 1/4 cup chopped onion
- 1 clove garlic, minced
- 1 tablespoon olive oil
- 1 teaspoon dried oregano
- 1/4 teaspoon salt
- 1/4 teaspoon black pepper

Directions:

1. Rinse rice in a fine-mesh strainer and place in the air fryer basket.
2. Add water, diced tomatoes, onion, garlic, olive oil, oregano, salt, and black pepper to the basket.
3. Stir the mixture and smooth it out evenly in the basket.
4. Set the air fryer to 350°F (175°C) and cook for 20 minutes.
5. Once the timer goes off, remove the basket from the air fryer and fluff the rice with a fork before serving.

Nutritional information: 238 calories, 4g protein, 42g carbohydrates, 6g fat, 2g fiber, 0mg cholesterol, 318mg sodium, 95mg potassium.

Oregano and Onion Bulgur

Yield: 2 servings | **Prep time:** 10 minutes | **Cook time:** 20 minutes

Ingredients:

- 1 cup bulgur wheat
- 1 1/2 cups vegetable broth
- 1 cup chopped kale
- 1/2 cup diced tomatoes
- 1/4 cup chopped red onion
- 1 tablespoon olive oil
- 1/2 teaspoon dried oregano
- Salt and pepper to taste

Directions:

1. Preheat the air fryer to 375°F (190°C).
2. Rinse the bulgur wheat and drain well.
3. In a bowl, mix the bulgur wheat with vegetable broth, olive oil, dried oregano, and salt and pepper to taste.
4. Place the mixture into the air fryer basket and cook for 10 minutes.
5. Stir in the kale, tomatoes, and red onion, and continue to cook for another 10 minutes, or until the bulgur is tender and the kale is slightly crispy.
6. Serve hot.

Nutritional information: 335 calories, 11g protein, 58g carbohydrates, 7g fat, 15g fiber, 0mg cholesterol, 322mg sodium, 649mg potassium.

Garlic Bulgur

Yield: 2 servings | **Prep time:** 10 minutes | **Cook time:** 20 minutes

Ingredients:

- 1 cup bulgur
- 1 medium zucchini, sliced
- 1 small onion, chopped
- 2 cloves garlic, minced
- 2 tbsp olive oil
- 1 tsp dried oregano
- Salt and black pepper to taste
- 1 1/2 cups water

Directions:

1. Rinse the bulgur under cold water and drain well.
2. In a mixing bowl, combine the bulgur, zucchini, onion, garlic, olive oil, oregano, salt, and black pepper.
3. Toss to mix everything together.
4. Preheat the air fryer to 360°F.
5. Add the bulgur mixture to the air fryer basket and spread it out evenly.
6. Pour water over the mixture.
7. Cook for 20 minutes or until the bulgur is tender, stirring occasionally.

Nutritional information: 321 calories, 8g protein, 48g carbohydrates, 11g fat, 13g fiber, 0mg cholesterol, 8mg sodium, 586mg potassium.

Cumin Buckwheat

Yield: 2 servings | **Prep time:** 10 minutes | **Cook time:** 15 minutes

Ingredients:

- 1/2 cup buckwheat
- 1 cup water
- 1/2 cup plain Greek yogurt
- 1/4 cup chopped fresh parsley
- 2 tbsp olive oil
- 1/2 tsp garlic powder
- 1/2 tsp ground cumin
- Salt and pepper to taste

Directions:

1. Rinse the buckwheat under cold water and drain.
2. Add the water and rinsed buckwheat to the air fryer basket and cook at 350°F for 10 minutes, shaking the basket occasionally.
3. In a small bowl, mix together the Greek yogurt, chopped parsley, olive oil, garlic powder, cumin, salt, and pepper.
4. When the buckwheat is done, transfer it to a serving bowl and top with the yogurt mixture. Serve warm or at room temperature.

Nutritional information: 315 calories, 13g protein, 36g carbohydrates, 13g fat, 5g fiber, 4mg cholesterol, 55mg sodium, 405mg potassium.

Bell Peppers Pilaf

Yield: 2 servings | **Prep time:** 10 minutes | **Cook time:** 20 minutes

Ingredients:

- 1/2 cup quinoa
- 1/2 cup bulgur
- 1 tbsp olive oil
- 1 onion, chopped
- 2 garlic cloves, minced
- 1/2 red bell pepper, chopped
- 1/2 zucchini, chopped
- 1/2 tsp dried oregano
- Salt and pepper, to taste

Directions:

1. Rinse quinoa and bulgur in a fine mesh sieve and set aside.
2. Preheat air fryer to 350°F.
3. In a large bowl, mix together olive oil, onion, garlic, red bell pepper, zucchini, oregano, salt, and pepper.
4. Add quinoa and bulgur to the bowl and mix until everything is well combined.
5. Transfer the mixture to the air fryer basket and cook for 20 minutes, stirring halfway through.
6. Once the pilaf is cooked, serve immediately and enjoy!

Nutritional information: 316 calories, 9g protein, 51g carbohydrates, 8g fat, 10g fiber, 0mg cholesterol, 295mg sodium, 738mg potassium.

Tender Quinoa

Yield: 2 servings | **Prep time:** 5 minutes | **Cook time:** 15 minutes

Ingredients:

- 1/2 cup quinoa
- 1 cup water
- 1/4 teaspoon salt
- 1/4 teaspoon black pepper
- 1/4 cup sliced almonds
- 1 tablespoon olive oil
- 1/4 teaspoon garlic powder

Directions:

1. Rinse quinoa thoroughly in a fine-mesh strainer and transfer to a bowl.
2. Add water, salt, and black pepper to the bowl and stir.
3. Preheat the air fryer to 350°F (175°C) for 3 minutes.
4. Add the quinoa mixture to the air fryer basket and cook for 10 minutes.
5. In a separate bowl, mix sliced almonds, olive oil, and garlic powder.
6. Add the almond mixture to the quinoa and stir.
7. Cook for another 5 minutes until the quinoa is crispy and the almonds are toasted.

Nutritional information: 252 calories, 8g protein, 28g carbohydrates, 12g fat, 4g fiber, 0mg cholesterol, 303mg sodium, 286mg potassium.

Paprika Quinoa Balls

Yield: 4 servings | **Prep time:** 20 minutes | **Cook time:** 15 minutes

Ingredients:

- 1/2 cup uncooked quinoa
- 1 cup water
- 1/2 cup chopped onion
- 1/2 cup chopped red bell pepper
- 1/4 cup chopped parsley
- 2 cloves garlic, minced
- 1/2 teaspoon ground cumin
- 1/2 teaspoon paprika
- 1/4 teaspoon salt
- 1/4 teaspoon black pepper
- 1-pound ground turkey
- Cooking spray

Directions:

1. Rinse quinoa and add it to a saucepan with water. Bring to a boil, then reduce heat and simmer for 15-20 minutes, until quinoa is cooked and water is absorbed.
2. In a large bowl, mix together cooked quinoa, onion, red bell pepper, parsley, garlic, cumin, paprika, salt, and black pepper. Add ground turkey and mix well.
3. Using your hands, form the mixture into small meatballs, about 1 tablespoon each.
4. Preheat the air fryer to 375°F. Spray the air fryer basket with cooking spray.
5. Place the meatballs in the air fryer basket and cook for 10-12 minutes, flipping them halfway through, until they are browned and cooked through.
6. Serve the meatballs with your favorite dipping sauce or on top of a salad.

Nutritional information: 273 calories, 25g protein, 16g carbohydrates, 12g fat, 2g fiber, 92mg cholesterol, 248mg sodium, 374mg potassium.

Garlic Sorghum

Yield: 2 servings | **Prep time:** 5 minutes | **Cook time:** 15 minutes

Ingredients:

- 1/2 cup sorghum
- 1 tbsp olive oil
- 1/2 tsp smoked paprika
- 1/2 tsp garlic powder
- 1/4 tsp sea salt
- Freshly ground black pepper, to taste
- Lemon wedges, for serving

Directions:

1. Rinse the sorghum and place it in a bowl. Cover it with 2 cups of water and soak it overnight or for at least 4 hours.
2. Drain the soaked sorghum and rinse it under cold water. Pat dry with a paper towel.
3. Preheat the air fryer to 375°F (190°C).
4. In a bowl, mix together the sorghum, olive oil, smoked paprika, garlic powder, sea salt, and black pepper until the sorghum is evenly coated.
5. Transfer the seasoned sorghum to the air fryer basket and cook for 15 minutes, shaking the basket every 5 minutes to ensure even cooking.
6. Once the sorghum is golden brown and crispy, remove it from the air fryer and let it cool for a few minutes.
7. Serve the roasted sorghum with lemon wedges on the side.

Nutritional information: 160 calories, 2g protein, 27g carbohydrates, 5g fat, 3g fiber, 0mg cholesterol, 150mg sodium, 110mg potassium.

Parsley Farro

Yield: 2 servings | **Prep time:** 5 minutes | **Cook time:** 18 minutes

Ingredients:

- 1/2 cup farro
- 1/2 cup cherry tomatoes, halved
- 1/4 cup crumbled feta cheese
- 1/4 cup chopped fresh parsley
- 1/4 cup chopped red onion
- 1 tablespoon extra-virgin olive oil
- Salt and black pepper to taste

Directions:

1. Rinse the farro under cold water and add it to the air fryer basket.
2. Add the cherry tomatoes, feta cheese, parsley, and red onion to the basket.
3. Drizzle the olive oil over the ingredients and season with salt and black pepper.
4. Toss everything together until well combined.
5. Air fry at 375°F (190°C) for 15-18 minutes or until the farro is tender and the vegetables are roasted.
6. Serve hot and enjoy!

Nutritional information: 270 calories, 10g protein, 36g carbohydrates, 10g fat, 6g fiber, 20mg cholesterol, 260mg sodium, 330mg potassium.

Cheese Buckwheat

Yield: 2 servings | **Prep time:** 10 minutes | **Cook time:** 20 minutes

Ingredients:

- 1 cup buckwheat
- 2 cups water
- 1/2 teaspoon salt
- 1/4 teaspoon black pepper
- 1/2 cup cherry tomatoes, halved
- 1/2 cup chopped cucumber
- 1/4 cup chopped fresh parsley
- 6 ounces Halloumi cheese, sliced

Directions:

1. Rinse the buckwheat in cold water and drain. Add the buckwheat, water, salt, and black pepper to a pot and bring to a boil. Reduce heat, cover and simmer for 15-20 minutes or until the water is absorbed and the buckwheat is tender.
2. In a medium bowl, combine the cooked buckwheat, cherry tomatoes, cucumber, and parsley. Mix well.
3. Preheat the air fryer to 375°F.
4. Place the sliced Halloumi cheese in the air fryer basket and cook for 5-7 minutes or until golden brown, flipping halfway through.
5. Serve the buckwheat mixture topped with the air fried Halloumi cheese.

Nutritional information: 449 calories, 26g protein, 50g carbohydrates, 17g fat, 7g fiber, 57mg cholesterol, 1043mg sodium, 462mg potassium.

Vegan Pilaf

Yield: 2 servings | **Prep time:** 10 minutes | **Cook time:** 20 minutes

Ingredients:

- 1 cup cremini mushrooms, sliced
- 1/2 cup brown rice
- 1/2 onion, chopped
- 1 clove garlic, minced
- 1 1/2 cups chicken or vegetable broth
- 1 tablespoon olive oil
- Salt and pepper to taste
- Optional: chopped parsley for garnish

Directions:

1. Preheat the air fryer to 375°F (190°C).
2. In a large bowl, mix together the mushrooms, rice, onion, garlic, olive oil, salt, and pepper.
3. Pour the mixture into the air fryer basket and spread it out evenly.
4. Pour the broth over the mixture.
5. Cook in the air fryer for 20 minutes, or until the rice is cooked and the liquid has been absorbed.
6. Garnish with chopped parsley, if desired.

Nutritional information: 256 calories, 6g protein, 40g carbohydrates, 8g fat, 4g fiber, 0mg cholesterol, 655mg sodium, 352mg potassium.

Tender Rice and Beef Balls

Yield: 2 servings | **Prep time:** 15 minutes | **Cook time:** 20 minutes

Ingredients:

- 1/2 lb. ground beef
- 1/2 cup cooked rice
- 1/4 cup chopped onion
- 1/4 cup chopped parsley
- 1 egg
- 1/4 cup bread crumbs
- 1 tsp. salt
- 1/2 tsp. black pepper
- Olive oil spray

Directions:

- In a large mixing bowl, combine ground beef, cooked rice, chopped onion, chopped parsley, egg, bread crumbs, salt, and black pepper. Mix until well combined.
- Form the mixture into 1-inch meatballs.
- Preheat the air fryer to 375°F.
- Spray the air fryer basket with olive oil.
- Place the meatballs in the air fryer basket in a single layer, making sure to leave some space between each meatball.
- Spray the top of the meatballs with olive oil.
- Air fry the meatballs for 10 minutes, then flip them over.
- Spray the other side of the meatballs with olive oil and air fry for another 10 minutes, or until they are golden brown and cooked through.
- Serve hot.

Nutritional information: 420 calories, 29g protein, 25g carbohydrates, 22g fat, 1g fiber, 140mg cholesterol, 990mg sodium, 400mg potassium.

Onion and Mushrooms Quinoa

Yield: 2 servings | **Prep time:** 10 minutes | **Cook time:** 18 minutes

Ingredients:

- 1 cup sliced mushrooms
- 1/2 cup quinoa
- 1/2 cup diced tomatoes
- 1/4 cup chopped onion
- 2 cloves garlic, minced
- 2 tablespoons chopped fresh parsley
- 1 tablespoon olive oil
- 1/2 teaspoon ground cumin
- Salt and pepper to taste

Directions:

1. Preheat the air fryer to 375°F (190°C).
2. In a mixing bowl, toss the mushrooms with olive oil, salt, and pepper.
3. Place the mushrooms in the air fryer basket and cook for 5 minutes, shaking the basket halfway through the cooking time.
4. In another mixing bowl, stir together the quinoa, diced tomatoes, chopped onion, minced garlic, chopped parsley, ground cumin, salt, and pepper.

5. Remove the mushrooms from the air fryer and add them to the quinoa mixture. Stir to combine.
6. Add the quinoa mixture to the air fryer basket and cook for 12-13 minutes, stirring occasionally, until the quinoa is cooked and the vegetables are tender.
7. Serve hot.

Nutritional information: 283 calories, 9g protein, 36g carbohydrates, 11g fat, 6g fiber, 0mg cholesterol, 163mg sodium, 547mg potassium.

Paprika Bulgur

Yield: 2 servings | **Prep time:** 10 minutes | **Cook time:** 20 minutes

Ingredients:

- 2 boneless, skinless chicken breasts
- 1/2 cup bulgur
- 1/2 cup chicken broth
- 1/2 onion, chopped
- 1/2 red bell pepper, chopped
- 2 cloves garlic, minced
- 1 teaspoon paprika
- Salt and black pepper, to taste
- Olive oil cooking spray

Directions:

1. Preheat the air fryer to 375°F (190°C).
2. Season the chicken breasts with paprika, salt, and black pepper.
3. Spray the air fryer basket with olive oil cooking spray and place the chicken breasts inside.
4. Cook the chicken in the air fryer for 10 minutes, then flip and cook for an additional 5-7 minutes, until the internal temperature reaches 165°F (74°C).
5. Remove the chicken from the air fryer and let it rest for a few minutes before slicing it into strips.
6. In the meantime, cook the bulgur according to package instructions, using chicken broth instead of water for added flavor.
7. Spray a non-stick skillet with olive oil cooking spray and sauté the onion, red bell pepper, and garlic over medium heat until softened, about 5-7 minutes.
8. Add the cooked bulgur to the skillet and mix well with the vegetables.
9. Serve the sliced chicken over the bulgur mixture.

Nutritional information: 325 calories, 30g protein, 31g carbohydrates, 8g fat, 6g fiber, 65mg cholesterol, 345mg sodium, 540mg potassium.

Cumin Balls

Yield: 2 servings | **Prep time:** 10 minutes | **Cook time:** 15 minutes

Ingredients:

- 1 cup cooked bulgur
- 1/2 cup chickpeas, mashed
- 1/4 cup finely chopped onion
- 1/4 cup finely chopped parsley
- 1 tablespoon lemon juice
- 1 teaspoon ground cumin
- Salt and pepper to taste
- 1/4 cup all-purpose flour
- Cooking spray

Directions:

1. In a mixing bowl, combine the cooked bulgur, mashed chickpeas, onion, parsley, lemon juice, cumin, salt, and pepper. Mix well.
2. Shape the mixture into small balls, about 1 1/2-inch in diameter.
3. Place the flour in a shallow dish and roll each ball in the flour to coat evenly.
4. Preheat the air fryer to 370°F.
5. Spray the air fryer basket with cooking spray and place the bulgur balls in a single layer in the basket.
6. Cook for 10-15 minutes, flipping the balls halfway through, until they are golden brown and crispy on the outside.
7. Serve with your favorite dipping sauce.

Nutritional information: 230 calories, 8g protein, 44g carbohydrates, 2g fat, 9g fiber, 0mg cholesterol, 105mg sodium, 472mg potassium.

Thyme Rice

Yield: 2 servings | **Prep time:** 10 minutes | **Cook time:** 25 minutes

Ingredients:

- 2 boneless, skinless chicken breasts
- 1/2 cup uncooked basmati rice
- 1/2 cup chicken broth
- 1/4 cup diced red onion
- 1/4 cup diced red bell pepper
- 2 cloves garlic, minced
- 1 tsp dried oregano
- 1 tsp dried thyme
- 1/4 tsp salt
- 1/4 tsp black pepper
- 1 tbsp olive oil

Directions:

1. Preheat the air fryer to 360°F (180°C).
2. In a mixing bowl, combine the uncooked rice, chicken broth, diced red onion, diced red bell pepper, minced garlic, dried oregano, dried thyme, salt, and black pepper. Mix well.
3. Pour the rice mixture into the air fryer basket and spread it out evenly.
4. Brush the chicken breasts with olive oil and place them on top of the rice mixture in the air fryer basket.
5. Air fry for 20-25 minutes or until the chicken is cooked through and the rice is tender.
6. Remove from the air fryer and allow the chicken to rest for 5 minutes before slicing and serving with the rice.

Nutritional information: 333 calories, 28g protein, 32g carbohydrates, 9g fat, 2g fiber, 66mg cholesterol, 488mg sodium, 389mg potassium.

Berries Quinoa

Yield: 2 servings | **Prep time:** 10 minutes | **Cook time:** 20 minutes

Ingredients:

- 1/2 cup uncooked quinoa
- 1 cup water
- 1/2 cup chopped strawberries
- 1/4 cup crumbled feta cheese
- 1 tablespoon chopped fresh mint
- 1 tablespoon olive oil
- Salt and pepper, to taste

Directions:

1. Rinse the quinoa in a fine mesh strainer and drain well.
2. In a medium-sized saucepan, bring the water to a boil over high heat. Add the quinoa and stir. Reduce the heat to low and cover the saucepan with a tight-fitting lid. Cook for 15-20 minutes or until the quinoa is tender and the water is absorbed.
3. In a mixing bowl, combine the cooked quinoa, chopped strawberries, crumbled feta cheese, chopped fresh mint, and olive oil. Toss well to combine.
4. Preheat the air fryer to 390°F (200°C).
5. Place the quinoa mixture in the air fryer basket and spread it out into an even layer.
6. Air fry for 5-7 minutes or until the strawberries are slightly caramelized and the quinoa is crispy.
7. Season with salt and pepper to taste.
8. Serve hot or at room temperature.

Nutritional information: 295 calories, 9g protein, 35g carbohydrates, 13g fat, 5g fiber, 17mg cholesterol, 178mg sodium, 344mg potassium.

Beans

Onion Beans

Yield: 2 servings | **Prep time:** 5 minutes | **Cook time:** 15 minutes

Ingredients:

- 1 can of mixed beans, drained and rinsed
- 1 red bell pepper, sliced
- 1 small red onion, sliced
- 1 tablespoon of olive oil
- 1 teaspoon of dried oregano
- Salt and black pepper, to taste

Directions:

1. Preheat the air fryer to 375°F (190°C).
2. In a bowl, mix the mixed beans, sliced red bell pepper, and sliced red onion together.
3. Drizzle olive oil over the mixture and toss to coat evenly.
4. Sprinkle dried oregano, salt, and black pepper over the mixture and toss again.
5. Place the mixture in the air fryer basket and cook for 15 minutes, shaking the basket every 5 minutes to ensure even cooking.
6. When done, remove the basket from the air fryer and let it cool for a few minutes before serving.

Nutritional information: 239 calories, 10g protein, 35g carbohydrates, 7g fat, 11g fiber, 0mg cholesterol, 394mg sodium, 697mg potassium.

Peppers and Beans Mix

Yield: 2 servings | **Prep time:** 10 minutes | **Cook time:** 15 minutes

Ingredients:

- 1 can of mixed beans, drained and rinsed
- 1 small red onion, diced
- 1 red bell pepper, diced
- 1 tablespoon of olive oil
- 1/2 teaspoon of dried oregano
- 1/2 teaspoon of smoked paprika
- Salt and pepper to taste

Directions:

1. Preheat the air fryer to 390°F.
2. In a mixing bowl, combine the mixed beans, diced red onion, and diced red bell pepper.
3. Drizzle the olive oil over the mixture and toss to coat evenly.
4. Add the dried oregano, smoked paprika, salt, and pepper to the mixing bowl and toss again to combine.
5. Transfer the bean mixture to the air fryer basket and spread it out into a single layer.
6. Air fry for 12-15 minutes, tossing halfway through the cooking time, until the beans are crispy and the vegetables are tender.
7. Serve hot as a side dish or as a filling for tacos, burritos, or bowls.

Nutritional information: 231 calories, 9g protein, 32g carbohydrates, 8g fat, 10g fiber, 0mg cholesterol, 291mg sodium, 747mg potassium.

Thyme Beans

Yield: 2 servings | **Prep time:** 10 minutes | **Cook time:** 15 minutes

Ingredients:

- 1 can (15 oz) cannellini beans, drained and rinsed
- 1 tbsp olive oil
- 1 tbsp chopped fresh rosemary
- 1 tbsp chopped fresh thyme
- 1/4 tsp salt
- 1/4 tsp black pepper
- 1 garlic clove, minced

Directions:

1. In a mixing bowl, toss the cannellini beans with olive oil, rosemary, thyme, salt, pepper, and minced garlic.
2. Preheat the air fryer to 400°F (200°C) for 5 minutes.
3. Spread the seasoned beans evenly in the air fryer basket and cook for 12-15 minutes, shaking the basket every 5 minutes or so, until the beans are crispy and golden brown.
4. Serve the herbed beans as a side dish or a light meal.

Nutritional information: 157 calories, 7g protein, 19g carbohydrates, 6g fat, 6g fiber, 0mg cholesterol, 295mg sodium, 404mg potassium.

Honey Snap Peas

Yield: 2 servings | **Prep time:** 5 minutes | **Cook time:** 8 minutes

Ingredients:

- 1 lb fresh sugar snap peas, trimmed
- 1 tbsp olive oil
- 1 tbsp soy sauce
- 1 tsp grated fresh ginger
- 1 tsp honey
- 1/4 tsp garlic powder

Directions:

1. Preheat the air fryer to 400°F (200°C).
2. In a medium bowl, whisk together the olive oil, soy sauce, ginger, honey, and garlic powder.
3. Add the trimmed sugar snap peas to the bowl and toss until coated.
4. Transfer the sugar snap peas to the air fryer basket and cook for 8 minutes, shaking the basket halfway through, until the peas are crisp-tender and slightly charred.
5. Serve immediately.

Nutritional information: 102 calories, 4g protein, 11g carbohydrates, 5g fat, 3g fiber, 0mg cholesterol, 442mg sodium, 318mg potassium.

Greek Style White Beans

Yield: 2 servings | **Prep time:** 10 minutes | **Cook time:** 15 minutes

Ingredients:

- 1 can (15 oz) of white beans, drained and rinsed
- 1/4 cup crumbled feta cheese
- 1/4 cup chopped Kalamata olives
- 1/4 cup chopped red onion
- 2 tablespoons chopped fresh parsley
- 1 tablespoon olive oil

Directions:

1. In a medium bowl, combine the white beans, feta cheese, Kalamata olives, red onion, parsley, and olive oil.
2. Mix well until the ingredients are evenly distributed.
3. Preheat the air fryer to 375°F.
4. Transfer the mixture to the air fryer basket and spread it out in an even layer.
5. Air fry for 15 minutes, shaking the basket occasionally to ensure even cooking.
6. Serve hot and enjoy!

Nutritional information: 282 calories, 13g protein, 22g carbohydrates, 16g fat, 7g fiber, 33mg cholesterol, 706mg sodium, 598mg potassium.

Olives and Beans

Yield: 2 servings | **Prep time:** 10 minutes | **Cook time:** 20 minutes

Ingredients:

- 1 can (15 oz) cannellini beans, drained and rinsed
- 1/4 cup chopped sun-dried tomatoes
- 1/4 cup chopped Kalamata olives
- 1/4 cup chopped red onion
- 2 cloves garlic, minced
- 1 tbsp olive oil
- 1 tsp dried oregano
- Salt and pepper to taste

Directions:

1. Preheat the air fryer to 390°F (200°C).
2. In a mixing bowl, combine the beans, sun-dried tomatoes, Kalamata olives, red onion, garlic, olive oil, oregano, salt, and pepper. Mix well.
3. Transfer the mixture to the air fryer basket and spread it out evenly.
4. Air fry for 10 minutes, then toss the mixture and continue air frying for an additional 10 minutes or until the beans are crispy and golden brown.
5. Serve hot as a side dish or a main meal.

Nutritional information: 285 calories, 12g protein, 30g carbohydrates, 13g fat, 8g fiber, 0mg cholesterol, 516mg sodium, 680mg potassium.

Tender Bean Mash

Yield: 2 servings | **Prep time:** 10 minutes | **Cook time:** 20 minutes

Ingredients:

- 1/2 cup dried white beans, soaked overnight
- 1/4 cup chopped onion
- 1 clove garlic, minced
- 1 tablespoon olive oil
- 2 cups water
- 1/2 teaspoon salt
- 1/4 teaspoon black pepper
- 1/4 teaspoon ground cumin

Directions:

1. Rinse the soaked white beans and drain them.
2. In a mixing bowl, toss the beans, onion, garlic, olive oil, salt, black pepper, and cumin until well coated.
3. Preheat the air fryer to 390°F (199°C).
4. Spread the bean mixture in a single layer in the air fryer basket.
5. Cook for 20 minutes, shaking the basket every 5 minutes to ensure even cooking.
6. Once the beans are tender and slightly crispy, remove from the air fryer and serve hot.

Nutritional information: 246 calories, 11g protein, 38g carbohydrates, 6g fat, 11g fiber, 0mg cholesterol, 304mg sodium, 731mg potassium.

Oregano Cannellini Beans

Yield: 2 servings | **Prep time:** 10 minutes | **Cook time:** 12 minutes

Ingredients:

- 1 can of cannellini beans, drained and rinsed
- 1 tablespoon of olive oil
- 2 cloves of garlic, minced
- 1 teaspoon of dried oregano
- 1/2 teaspoon of salt
- 1/4 teaspoon of black pepper

Directions:

1. Preheat the air fryer to 400°F.
2. In a mixing bowl, combine the beans, olive oil, minced garlic, dried oregano, salt, and black pepper. Toss to coat the beans evenly.
3. Transfer the seasoned beans to the air fryer basket and cook for 12 minutes, shaking the basket halfway through cooking.
4. Once done, remove the beans from the air fryer and serve hot.

Nutritional information: 165 calories, 7g protein, 19g carbohydrates, 8g fat, 6g fiber, 0mg cholesterol, 595mg sodium, 310mg potassium.

Paprika Black Beans Ragout

Yield: 2 servings | **Prep time:** 10 minutes | **Cook time:** 20 minutes

Ingredients:

- 1 can (15 oz) black beans, drained and rinsed
- 1/2 onion, chopped
- 2 cloves garlic, minced
- 1 red bell pepper, chopped
- 1 teaspoon ground cumin
- 1 teaspoon smoked paprika
- Salt and pepper to taste
- 1 tablespoon olive oil
- 1/2 cup vegetable broth

Directions:

1. Preheat the air fryer to 375°F.
2. In a mixing bowl, add black beans, onion, garlic, red bell pepper, cumin, smoked paprika, salt, pepper, and olive oil. Mix well.
3. Transfer the mixture to the air fryer basket and spread it evenly.
4. Pour the vegetable broth over the bean mixture.
5. Cook for 20 minutes, stirring halfway through the cooking time.
6. Serve hot and enjoy!

Nutritional information: 184 calories, 9g protein, 27g carbohydrates, 5g fat, 9g fiber, 0mg cholesterol, 485mg sodium, 554mg potassium.

Tomato Beans

Yield: 2 servings | **Prep time:** 10 minutes | **Cook time:** 20 minutes

Ingredients:

- 1 can (15 oz) of cannellini beans, drained and rinsed
- 2 celery stalks, sliced
- 1/4 cup diced onion
- 1/4 cup diced tomato
- 2 cloves garlic, minced
- 1/4 tsp dried oregano
- Salt and black pepper to taste
- 2 tbsp olive oil

Directions:

1. Preheat the air fryer to 375°F.
2. In a bowl, mix the beans, celery, onion, tomato, garlic, oregano, salt, pepper, and olive oil until well combined.
3. Transfer the mixture to the air fryer basket and spread it out in an even layer.
4. Air fry for 20 minutes, stirring occasionally, until the celery is tender and the beans are lightly browned.
5. Serve hot as a side dish or over rice.

Nutritional information: 272 calories, 8g protein, 32g carbohydrates, 13g fat, 8g fiber, 0mg cholesterol, 404mg sodium, 719mg potassium.

Copyright © 2023 by Emmett Carlson.

All rights reserved. No part of this cookbook may be reproduced, distributed, or transmitted in any form or by any means, including photocopying, recording, or other electronic or mechanical methods, without the prior written permission of the author, except in the case of brief quotations embodied in critical reviews and certain other noncommercial uses permitted by copyright law.

The recipes and advice presented in this cookbook are intended for informational purposes only. The author is not a licensed dietitian, and the information contained in this cookbook should not be considered a substitute for professional medical advice, diagnosis, or treatment. The author disclaims any liability or responsibility for any loss or damage caused or alleged to be caused, directly or indirectly, by the use or misuse of any information contained in this cookbook.

By using this cookbook, you acknowledge that you have read and understand the information presented in this copyright and disclaimer statement, and you agree to be bound by the terms and conditions set forth herein.

Made in the USA
Las Vegas, NV
15 September 2023